Hold On

THE LIGHT WILL COME

AND OTHER
LESSONS MY
SONGS HAVE
TAUGHT ME

MICHAEL McLEAN

SHADOW
MOUNTAIN

Visit us at shadowmountain.com

Library of Congress Cataloging-in-Publication Data

McLean, Michael, 1952-
  Hold on, the light will come : and other lessons my songs have taught me / Michael McLean.
    p.   cm.
  ISBN 1-59038-088-6 (alk. paper)
  1. McLean, Michael, 1952- 2. McLean, Michael, 1952- Songs. 3. Contemporary Christian music—History and criticism. I. Title.
  ML410.M454 A3 2003
  782.42'171'0092—dc21   2003012444

Printed in the United States of America   72076-7110
Publishers Printing, Salt Lake City, UT

10 9 8 7 6 5 4 3 2 1

CONTENTS

ACKNOWLEDGMENTS

♪

This book is about the lessons my songs have taught me, but many of these songs would never have been written without the inspiration and creativity of some amazing collaborators: John Batdorf (who let me put lyrics to his melodies for "Let It Go," "It's Not Love," and "She's the Girl"), David Tinney (who wrote the melody for "It's Nice When Some Things Are Forgotten"), Bryce Neubert (who penned the tune for "The Man with Many Names"), Chris Harding (who was my co-writer on "Stay with Me"), and Kevin Kelly, who came up with the idea for our musical *The Ark*, which brought forth the title song of this book. From these gifted musicians and friends I discovered how the whole truly can become greater than the sum of the parts.

I also realize that there wouldn't be anything to write about if no one had ever given these songs a chance to heard, or encouraged the one who wrote them. Some of the people I most wish to thank and dedicate this book to are no longer with us: Merrill Bradshaw, a composition professor who told me on a critical, turning-point day in my life that if I were to quit writing songs he would consider it a personal loss; Elaine Cannon, who pushed for the song "You're Not Alone" to be sung at a satellite conference for women; my Grandma Nona, who taught me how to tell a story by telling so many wonderful ones of her own; my cousin Mark, whose life was one of the greatest compositions of all time; and every ancestor who contributed something to the gene pool that made me who I am.

Had my own mother not endured the practicing, the endless hunting and pecking for that perfect note, and then been such an insightful and enthusiastic audience, day or night, I never would have dared to share a song I had tried to write with anyone, anywhere. Had my wife and children not suffered through my emotional disappearances when the "juice was flowing," I'd never have been able to stay on task long enough to complete anything.

And had my unborn grandchildren not been calling to me to get these thoughts down before my memory completely escapes me, I'd never have felt compelled to talk about such personal and private things with the hope that such sharing might help others not feel so alone.

The people who have published and distributed so much of my work for the last twenty years deserve a special award for an unusual combination of support, encouragement, and patience. I am such a high-maintenance person and have been so lovingly indulged for such a long time.

Most of all, I'm indebted to the people who've taken their pizza, ice cream, and Big Gulp money and spent it on my music and words since 1983. Were it not for that support, I could never have given as much of my life to this endeavor as I have. It seems only fitting that I share the best stories of the adventure with those who bought my ticket.

—MICHAEL MCLEAN

INTRO

No offense, but I really hate your songs." Her warm and thoughtful greeting made me wonder why I'd ever been shy about becoming a songwriter.

"You know why, don't you?" the woman went on. "It's because everything works out for everybody in your songs. I just hate that. I know you're probably trying to be positive and nurturing, but your happily-ever-after songs depress me."

"Why?"

This was actually the second response that had come to my mind. My first, the obvious one: "Little low on Prozac, are we?" seemed a bit cold for a guy who'd built his career on being really sensitive.

"Why?" She was incensed. "You ask why? There's the problem right there—you just don't understand. When things work out in your songs but not in life it means that either your songs are wrong . . . or my life is."

It was sort of an awkward moment. She had me trapped between the Metabolife and the SlimFast cases waiting for the pharmacist to fill a prescription. I suppose I could have escaped, had I been thinking clearly, but being the pleaser that I am, I just stood there, my mind racing, desperately trying to think of a song that I'd written sometime in the last thirty years that was hopeless and depressing enough to comfort my fellow shopper.

"Did you ever hear 'No More Love'? Things don't work out at all in that song. The lyric goes, 'I got no more love to give you, I got no more time to spend/Emotionally I'm in bankruptcy/My heart's in chapter seven . . . '"

I started tapping my toe to give her a sense of the rhythm, and then I explained, "Originally, I wrote the line: 'Emotionally I'm in bankruptcy/My heart's in chapter eleven' because it fit the tune better. But then a lawyer told me that chapter eleven bankruptcy means that there's a plan to restructure and try again, whereas chapter seven means, 'Stick a fork in me, I'm done.'"

"That song's just a joke, and you know it."

I panicked. Surely there was a song I'd written that captured the dark side of life, offering no solutions, no spiritual editorializing, no hope, no restitution, no redemption, and absolutely no concern or comfort coming from heavenly hosts.

"Tell me something," she said. "Who do you think you're writing your songs for, anyway?"

It made me think. I didn't answer immediately because I wanted to tell the truth, and I think I discovered it as these words sort of poured out of me.

"Me. I'm writing these songs because I need them. I know life's hard and things are tough . . . I know how dark it can feel . . . why do you think I'm waiting in line for antidepressants? But when I hear a story in a song, and someone overcomes something, or finds a way to hold on or learns how to let go or discovers something that alters the way they view their life, I want to celebrate it. I want to hear it sung in the morning when I wake up and hum it back to myself as I go to sleep. I want to know that somewhere inside of me I'm capable of feeling hope . . . I suppose I write songs the way I do because sometimes a song can teach me the truth the only way my heart will hear it . . ."

"Mr. McLean? Your prescription is ready."

"Excuse me . . . I'm sure that's more than you ever wanted to know about a bunch of songs that you hate . . ."

She didn't say anything for a while. She looked like she felt sort of sorry for me.

Then she smiled. "Little low on Prozac, are we?"

"Celexa. Doesn't make me sleepy."

At that moment, somebody over in the electronics department cranked up a boom box, and for a few seconds everyone in the neighborhood could hear "I Can't Get No Satisfaction."

I nodded my head to the beat. "Sounds like they're playing your song," I shouted to the woman.

I remember her smiling as she walked away, singing along even after the stereo had been turned down . . .

I don't know if these introductory thoughts are meant to be a disclaimer, a warning, or an apology to those who may find the following stories and songs depressingly hopeful. I'd like you to know, if you choose to read on and possibly listen to the songs on the CD in the back of the book, that even though I wrote them, I don't love these songs as much as I love what they've taught me or as much as I love the people who inspired them.

Somewhere between holding on and letting go, between love lost and love found, between promises made and promises kept, between those who build us up and those who let us down, our lives are lived and our lessons are learned. And somewhere between the living and the learning a handful of songs came along like emotional signposts, reminding me where I'd been and showing me where it was possible to go. If it seems like there's something familiar about these musical landmarks, perhaps it is because you, too, have been to the places they came from.

CHAPTER 1

WHAT I NEED

𝄞

Halfway through my third-grade year, my family moved from Lawn Dale Drive to the corner of Harvard Avenue and Fourth East. The two addresses were three hundred miles and what seemed like an entire world apart. On Lawn Dale Drive I had friends; on Harvard Avenue I had relatives. On Lawn Dale Drive I played on the OK Food Center Jets Little League baseball team. On Harvard Avenue I played for Sorensen's Furnace Cleaners. That was our sponsor *and* our name. Not the Yankees or the Dodgers or the Braves or any generally accepted baseball team names. The Furnace Cleaners. The only thing that kept my fellow Furnace Cleaners from feeling too bad about it was the fact that the year before we were sponsored by Magical Chemical Toilet Supply. I'm not making this up.

When the other kids are on teams like Prudential Insurance or Safeway, and you're one of Sorensen's Furnace Cleaners, it can affect your self-esteem in not-so-subtle ways. You find yourself branded by an association you didn't even pick, and it rubs off on you. At age nine you're not grateful that somebody's dad ponied up the money so you could even have uniforms and be a team. You just think the baseball gods have decided to play a cruel joke on you because you deserve it.

To counter the low self-esteem, I found myself searching for anything and everything I could find that would build me up somehow. It was tough finding that magic esteem-building thing because I wasn't really very good at anything. And then someone magical moved in next door.

He was a concert pianist who looked to me like Clark Kent, but I could see past the glasses and I knew he was really Superman. Any who doubted that changed their minds when they heard him play Liszt. He was so incredibly cool, he made classical music more exciting than Elvis singin' rock 'n' roll. Not only did he play the piano with the skill and passion of a Greek god, he wasn't a wimp in the rest of his life. He jumped out of airplanes for the National Guard. He had strong arms and even stronger hands and a pretty wife, and he became my piano teacher.

At my first piano lesson, my hero teacher told me that I had music inside of me that was just aching to get out, and that the only reason people put up with the pain of practicing the piano was so they could let that music out. He gave me an example of what he was talking about.

"Suppose you're feeling sad," he said, "and you want to express that sadness before it eats you alive inside." Then he played a haunting passage from Chopin that almost made me cry.

"Or maybe you're angry or frustrated or just plain mad. It'll kill you if you keep those feelings locked up." Then my hero piano teacher played an extremely intense piece by Beethoven.

"And what do you do if you're just so happy you think you'll explode?"

I would have said something about running over to the park and playing baseball with my friends, but sitting on that piano bench next to my teacher, all I could think of was how great it would be if I could express my joy in music the way he could.

He started playing an exciting piece that felt like pure melodic joy. Then he said, "You've got all that music locked up in you."

"Really?" I couldn't imagine anything so wonderful being buried inside my nine-year-old frame, but if he said it was true, then it must be.

"Your hands are like the gates to a prison that keep the music locked inside, and learning how to play the piano is nothing more than unlocking the gates."

Being a military man, my teacher believed in discipline. Practicing scales with him was like going to boot camp for fingers. He was tough as nails and didn't let me get away with anything, but he was never mean or degrading. He just expected a lot, and it would have killed me to let him down.

The first piece we started working on was a Tarantella by Mendelssohn.

7

"Do you think a kid my age can play something like this?" I asked.

"No 'kid' music for you, Michael. There's nothing you can't tackle if you're willing to give it your all."

My definition of "giving it my all" at the age of nine was a bit different from my teacher's. We spent six weeks just on the left hand of the first page. Six more on the right, and three more putting them together—with feeling. It took something like eight months before I was able to play the entire piece, memorized, of course, and with the coloring that brought a smile to my teacher's face. Eight months for one piece. Seemed like a long time to work on a song that didn't last three minutes. The next one took almost a year. By the end of my second year of studying the piano I had three pieces I could play in public. What I lacked in quantity I made up for in style.

I didn't know a lot of other kids my age who were working on Rachmaninoff. (I could play it, never could spell it). It did *wonders* for my self-esteem, and it didn't hurt my baseball, either. Something about working hard at a task and seeing the results sort of spills over to everything else in your life.

The problem with playing a few difficult pieces really well at a young age is that people think you're really, really smart—some sort of prodigy who is destined for greatness. The other problem is that you start believing it's true.

I decided that I must be special in some way because nobody else my age within a seven-block radius of Harvard Avenue and Fourth East could even pronounce *Rachmaninoff*, let alone play his music. That was good enough for me. I set my sights on becoming a concert pianist. This lasted until my teacher took me to a concert featuring a world-class artist.

We sat in the box seats close to the front of the concert hall so we could see the pianist's fingers fly across the keyboard. It was spectacular. The performance was flawless, and the crowd went wild. But on the way home, something occurred to me. Someday, I thought, that amazing pianist would get old and his fingers wouldn't be able to play those melodies. Eventually the skillful technician would die, and his performances would fade from memory or possibly be forgotten altogether. But the music he had played wasn't going to die. It was immortal somehow. The one who writes the music lives longer than the one who plays it. These were the thoughts of my eleven-year-old brain.

My practicing changed after that. During those marathon sessions of perfecting one classical piece, I started improvising on the melodies created by the masters. What if Mozart had done this right here? What if Chopin had tried this? I played around with alternate tunes, only to discover why we loved the melodies as they had been written. But I was on a different path and had abandoned the dream of performing classical music on a concert stage. Rather, I thought I'd try to make a contribution that would outlive me. I tried writing songs.

My first song was about Sunday dinner. Not exactly a subject worthy of Beethoven or Brahms, but it was something I knew well and was willing to work with. I wrote this song during what may one day be referred to as my food fetish period.

The tune for the song wasn't much—half stolen from other melodies that had caught my eleven-year-old fancy. But the words are worth mentioning. They were inspired by my mother's Sunday dinners, which almost always consisted of roast beef, mashed potatoes and gravy, carrots and peas, and green Jell-O something. The fruit inside the gelatin varied from week to week, but the lettuce arrangement it sat on and the white topping were always the same.

Staring at that Sabbath tradition, I wrote these lyrics on a paper napkin next to my fork:

> 'Twas very, very gloomy for the carrots and peas that day.
> The potato dam had broken, and the gravy came rushing their way.
> Their coloring would be ruined;
> Their destiny would be
> Choking, coughing, drowning in that dark brown sea.
> But then, from up above,
> The big fork stabbed the meat,
> Heroically plugged up the dam—
> The peas didn't suffer defeat.

With the stunning success of my first song (I was asked to sing it the next week for my grandma) came a string of other hits. I rewrote the lyrics to Roger Miller's "King of the Road" for my Boy Scout Troop and followed that up with a Halloween trick-or-treat song that increased my candy-per-house ratio 400 percent. Next stop, immortality. I just needed to keep writing.

I wrote songs for everything from school pep assemblies to skits at church fund-raisers. I wrote songs of love for girls I had crushes on and songs of heartbreak when they didn't care if I ever sang to them. I wrote my teenage angst and my deepest feelings, and those songs became my friends and a part of my family.

Some of the songs were written at the piano, and others I composed with a guitar Santa brought me for Christmas, selected from the Sears and Roebuck catalog. I remember the nights when I would lock myself in the downstairs bathroom and sing my songs in front of the mirror. For some reason, I did that only on nights when my parents were out and I was baby-sitting my little sister and she was asleep . . . or at least I thought she was.

On one of those nights when my overly curly hair had a particularly cool wave in it, I sang my heart out into that mirror and dreamed of being a star, with thousands of fans who hung on every word and every chord of every song. I tried to plump my pillows in a position that would enable me to sleep all night without messing up my perfect hair. But, of course, it didn't work. In the cold light of day my hair kinked up like a wire ball, my songs didn't sound as cool as they had with the reverb of the bathroom, and the thousands of fans in the mirror were off doing something else, like going to school or hanging out with their friends.

It was in those moments—those vulnerable, real-life, who-am-I moments—that the best songs of my youth were born. These were the songs that comforted me and talked back to me, that let me know I wasn't alone.

Over the course of the next thirty-five years, a little part of me always thought the dreams I'd dreamed while singing to the mirror

11

in the bathroom would come true. I would be a major talent on a big-time record label with a gazillion adoring fans. Didn't happen the way I dreamed. I've found some friends who have let my music be a part of their lives, and they've been kind enough to buy enough copies to help me pay the bills so I can work on more of those real-life, vulnerable, who-am-I songs. I'm grateful beyond words that I didn't become the star I dreamed of being, because a part of me knows it could have destroyed me. I've had the extraordinary blessing of getting not what I thought I wanted, but what I need.

All I ever wanted, all I ever dreamed of,
Everything I hoped, and all the things I prayed for
Couldn't hold a candle to what I've been given,
I've been given what I need.

CHAPTER 2

You're Not Alone

Twenty years ago I was working at an advertising agency trying to edit some of my unpublished three-minute songs of hope into thirty-second public service announcements. Not knowing what to do with all the songs that refused to fit the commercial-length format, I tried to talk a small independent book publisher and retailer into adding music to their repertoire—namely, mine. I knew that music wasn't their specialty, but wouldn't it be a natural fit to have some inspirational music sold alongside their inspirational books? Made sense to me. The publisher wasn't so sure.

The greatest concern was conceptual. I was pitching an album in which the "artist" was the songwriter. Several different singers would perform songs written by one songwriter. It was a bit of a stretch for a book publisher to release a musical album, but it was even harder to buy when the guy whose name was on the record wasn't the featured vocalist.

The working title of the album was *You're Not Alone*, taken from a song I'd written for a college friend who was going through a devastating divorce. For over three years I kept sellin' but nobody was buyin'. This was not just true of the bookstores but of several other entities as well. Companies I had written snappy little commercials for in the past weren't buying anything new. Old freelance clients weren't returning my phone calls. A screenplay I'd worked on for a couple of years wasn't ringing anybody's chimes. The production company I worked for wasn't sure what to do with me because my idea bank seemed overdrawn. I wasn't just having a hard time sellin' ideas—I couldn't *give* anything away!

I got so depressed with how things were going for me professionally that I went into hibernation mode. Took all my vacation and comp time and shut down. Didn't shave, didn't speak, didn't write, didn't sing, didn't do much of anything . . . except eat.

That's when I discovered fly-fishing.

My father-in-law had tried for years to get me enthused about the sport, but it had never appealed to me. I can't deny that fly fishermen looked pretty impressive in the magazines, but no one ever showed you what a person has to go through to get as good as the guy in the magazine. Fly-fishing was for people with too much time on their hands, nowhere else to go, and nothing else to do . . . wait a minute . . . that described me perfectly. So I headed for the Big Wood River in Idaho.

The appeal was threefold. One, it was beautiful. Two, my father-in-law tied his own flies and knew where the fish lived. And three, the room at the condo was free.

The first fish I ever caught wasn't very big, and I suspect it wasn't very smart, either, because I'd been slapping the water with my fly line and cussing pretty loudly when my line got tangled in the bushes behind me. Nevertheless, I did manage to get my No. 14 elk hair caddis out into the stream long enough to hook a scrappy little rainbow and reel him in.

It was a thrill, and I didn't exactly understand why. It certainly wasn't because of the pride I felt in making an exquisite cast. It wasn't because I'd tied my own fly and fooled a wily native trout. It wasn't because I'd read the river brilliantly and matched the hatch. It wasn't because I had caught dinner for my family. But it was a thrill just the same, and I loved that little fish. Before I placed him back in the stream, I kissed his nose and told him that we had a lot in common, he and I: We were both young and not too crafty in the ways of the world, but we should never attribute to stupidity that which could adequately be explained by hunger.

Though I didn't think of it at the time, it occurs to me now that maybe what I loved about that trout was that, in catching him, I didn't feel so alone. A fellow failure had snagged himself on my line, and we were bonded forever.

Regardless of what deep psychological rumblings were going on inside, I was hooked—pun intended—and came back to the condo with the tales of my expedition. I relived every cast, every strike, every happy moment I had spent that evening knee-deep in crystal clear water and bathing in blue sky and pine needles.

15

The next morning I raced to the fly-fishing shop and bought some hip boots and more accessories than a person with my skill level deserved. On the rest of the trip I didn't improve that much as a fisherman, but man, I looked like one. Seeing my bearded reflection in the window of the truck, all decked out in my hip boots, vest, and the finest fishing hat ever, I found a new identity: Fly-Master Mike, the River Roving Troubadour. I was singing again and didn't care who heard me. All was right with the world. I even felt like I could face my recent round of rejections, thanks to the rejuvenating power of a great trout stream.

It didn't last long. Three days after returning from Idaho, I was back in the same place I had been before I left, aware of my failures and unsure how to proceed. It was Saturday, and my escape route that day was a long nap in the basement. What woke me was a song.

Coming from the television in the family room was a tune that sounded instantly familiar . . . like the kind you turn the radio up for because you have a feeling you're going to like this one. The lyrics seemed simple enough, but they grabbed me in the gut. I was hooked, and the melody reeled me up from the basement into the family room.

A young woman with a beautiful voice was singing to a large audience of women, and the performance was being broadcast live, via satellite, to viewers throughout the world. My wife came over to me and gave me a hug. "Well, that ought to make you feel pretty special," she said. "Not every songwriter gets their song sung 'round the world."

It was "You're Not Alone." I was hearing that song for the first time not as the one who had written it, but as the one it was written for. I'd been caught, like a trout on a stream, by a song that filled a hunger deep inside.

Here's a little song to help you get along—
It will see you through when you're feeling blue.
And though it's not profound, when you're feeling down
So down
Sing this little tune and you'll feel better soon.
You're not alone, even though right now you're on your own.
You are loved in ways that can't be shown,
Your needs are known,
You're not alone.
And when you cry you're just letting go a heartache deep inside
So tomorrow there'll be sunshine and sky and love close by,
You're not alone.
Well, I know that it's not easy, but I know that it won't last,
'Cause one who loves you more than me
Is sending blessings fast—
You're not alone. Say it one more time, "I'm not alone."
And even when it's hard to find the words,
Your prayers are always heard.
You're not alone.

The following Monday morning I got a call from my friends at the book publishing company. Apparently a lot of women had connected with "You're Not Alone," just like I had, over the weekend. The publishers told me they'd been thinking a lot about my idea for an album and believed that the timing might be right for its release. I didn't disagree.

Had it not been for that broadcast and the willingness of a book company to take a chance on a songwriter who doesn't sing that well, I'd probably never have found the unique audience that has stuck with me through twenty-four albums, two books, three musicals, an oratorio, and now this. And I'm grateful, believe me I am . . . though at times I wonder, if the writing thing hadn't worked out, how I would have fared as a fishing guide.

CHAPTER 3

A Heart in the Right Place

The pressure was getting to me. I'd been asked to write a musical that would feature the talents of an amazingly gifted troupe of singers/dancers/actors who had won acclaim doing showstopping numbers from Broadway's greatest hits. The show's producers wanted something new and tailored to the talents of the cast, with production numbers that could outdazzle the Broadway review along with emotional pieces that would touch the heart. I was intimidated.

Oh, and I was working on a new collection of songs for a small, independent label, and it was following an album filled with the best songs I'd ever written. The label wanted something better.

And there was this one other thing going on. I was writing a Christmas movie for the production company I worked for, and the only reason I had this assignment was because a few years earlier I had produced a successful Christmas film for television starring

Jimmy Stewart and the Mormon Tabernacle Choir. It had been syndicated throughout the U.S. and around the world, had been seen by more than 300 million people and produced in several languages. "But," the production company asked me, "couldn't you do something a little deeper and more meaningful?"

Each project had deadlines, and they were looming *large!* A real sense of panic increased in me almost hourly. I started spending more time trying to get out of the assignments I'd worked so hard to earn than actually doing the work. Every day I had a knot in my stomach and the feeling that I'd already done the best I was ever going to do, and that trying again would simply reveal me as the fraud I knew I was.

Then I had an experience that radically changed my perspective and the way I approached my creative work. I had a conversation with some part of myself I don't think I had ever spoken to before. Now, I'm using words here, because that's all I have to describe this experience, but the questions came more in the form of thoughts than words, and I heard them with my heart, not my ears. Something inside asked me what seemed like a very random question. "Are you good?"

At first I ignored it.

The question, "Are you good?" wouldn't go away. It happened a second, third, and fourth time over the course of about an hour. I couldn't figure out what was going on inside, or what it meant. Was the question, "Am I good at what I do?" or, "Am I a good person?" I didn't understand.

This was all happening during a lengthy recording session in which things weren't going particularly well. The law of diminishing returns was setting in, so we called it a night, and I started the fifty-three-mile drive home. I popped in a tape of the work we'd done that evening to see if anything could be saved.

As I was driving home, that strange inner questioning surfaced again, but the question changed from, "Are you good?" to, "Who are you doing this for?"

I didn't have a clue what that meant any more than I had understood "Are you good?" But it felt less weird, this new question, and it made me think, "What am I doing *what* for?"

"Not what—*who*. The songs, the writing, the assignments . . . who are you doing this for?"

Why this questioning wouldn't leave me alone, I didn't understand, but I found myself engaged and responding to those inner thoughts. Who am I doing my creative work for? My wife, my kids, the bankers, the insurance salesmen, the credit card companies . . .

"This isn't that complicated. Tell the truth. Are you good? And who are you doing this for?"

Something inside wanted an answer, an absolutely honest one, and somehow I knew I couldn't lie.

"Truth? Truth is, I don't know if I'm any good. In fact, I'm filled with enough insecurities to fill Yankee Stadium in the off-season—"

My train of thought was interrupted: "Not *that* kind of good. This is about you as a person. Are you good? Deep down inside, where nobody but you can see, are you good?"

"I'm okay, I guess."

"But not good enough?"

"Probably not. I mean, I try my best, but sometimes I—"

"Stop right there. You try your best. One of these days you're going to learn how good enough that is. So, who are you doing what you're doing for?"

It was strange, but at that moment I knew again that lying was impossible. Exaggerating, which I'd made into an art form, was also out of the question. I wasn't frightened to tell the truth—in fact, I felt released from whatever prison my pretense had kept me in for far too long. I let the truth just spill out, and it came easily.

"I guess I do this for me. I want people to like me, and I want to feel like what I do makes a difference."

"Because . . ."

" . . . because then people will say *really* nice things about me and like me that much more."

"Thanks for being so honest with yourself."

"I didn't think I could lie."

"You couldn't, but just the same, it's wonderful when you just surrender to the truth."

After that sank in, the inner dialogue continued. I remember expressing to myself all kinds of fears. Fear of failing, and of having people find out that I'm really not very talented or very clever or creative or very . . . very . . . what's the word? *Worthy.* I realized I was afraid people would discover that I wasn't worthy of their praise, and they wouldn't like me.

"No wonder you've been so scared. How would you like that fear to go away?"

It's funny, but sometimes the thing we want most in life is the thing we're truly afraid of, for some reason. We're afraid it's not pos-sible, or that we'll be hurt if we believe in something that ultimately isn't true, so we give up before we begin. But on this particular evening, my hope for finding some inner peace was so great that I forged ahead.

"What do I need to do?"

The answer wasn't very complicated. I got the feeling that I needed to work on being as good as I could be as a human being. And on the days when being good didn't come as naturally as I would have liked, I didn't need to obsess over the failures, but rather get back on track and keep moving forward. (Why is it that all the obvious stuff seems so profound when you're finally in a place where you can receive it?)

After I'd considered what being good meant in my life, I won-dered what else needed my attention.

"Don't do what you're doing for you anymore. Do it for some-one else. Don't worry about building your kingdom—help the Lord build His."

As I read what I'm writing, it's sounding dangerously close to an evangelistic calling, and that's not what happened. It wasn't so much a calling as it was an invitation. At that moment, I even felt like it was one I could accept.

When I was about fifteen miles from home, all this inner dia-logue seemed to be summed up in these words: *If you're good, and you're doing what you're doing for somebody else, you won't fail.*

At nine miles from home the impression came with even

greater clarity and comfort: "If you're good, and you're doing what you're doing for somebody besides yourself, you won't fail. Promise."

"But how? How will I know if I'm doing it right?"

"You'll know."

At that, the conversation that had filled my drive home was over.

The next morning, my life without the compelling inner dialogue returned, as did the reality of my deadlines. Every day the pressure mounted. Before I felt I was ready, it was time to deliver. Try as I would to summon that inner voice for some reassurance, it didn't come. I finally concluded that I knew already what I needed to do, and so I met each day trying to be good and trying to do something for somebody else.

I didn't fail.

The new album was better than the previous one. The musical ran for five sold-out seasons, and the Christmas film worked just fine.

For me, it was a miracle, but because it happened in the natural course of events and with no small amount of work on my part, I began to forget how it had all come about.

Less than a year later, my record label noticed that I was selling a lot of albums and encouraged me to get a new one on the market soon. "We think you're hitting your stride, and this next record could really put you over the top. So get writing. We think you're a star on the rise."

Man, did I love hearing that: "We think you're a star on the rise." I thought about those words; I drenched myself in those

24

words; I propelled myself into the studio on the power of those words. I even ventured out of my little valley in the Intermountain West and cruised the neighborhoods of Malibu and Beverly Hills imagining the fitting location for a "star on the rise."

I started positioning myself—in my mind's eye, at least—as rising above the rest, and as someone who would have to be careful not to show on the outside what was happening on the inside. I spent a lot of time worrying about how to carry the burden of my rising star graciously. The best way to preserve the feeling of being special was to pretend that I didn't need it. Trying to apply a touch of modesty at the moments when I was receiving the most praise seemed to be working pretty well until a new crop of creative assignments eventually needed to be planted, and the pressure to deliver started mounting again.

It was then that I should have invented a video game called Deadline Dodger, patterned after the old Space Invaders game and marketed exclusively to creative people. I came up with excuses to miss meetings with my record company because I didn't have songs worth listening to. It wasn't for lack of trying. Day after day I put in the time, I studied the pop charts, I listened to the hits that other "stars on the rise" were recording and convinced myself that I could do that too. But nothing worked.

The day finally came when I couldn't postpone reality any longer. It was a late morning in the spring, and I was at my piano, working fruitlessly, trying to make a bad song seem good with a different arrangement. In frustration I finally pounded on the keyboard. I think I remember this happening in an old movie about some other "star on the rise" who couldn't find "his sound."

And then something deep inside that had been silent for a while ended its long stillness with a chuckle. I know this sounds a little weird, but I don't know how else to describe it. Something deep down was chuckling at me and causing me to think this thought: "Now, who are you doing all this for?"

I'd been caught. As powerfully as that moment struck me, its sharpness didn't come from a place filled with disappointment or anger or bitterness or rejection. Just clarity, and understanding, and love . . . and it was accompanied by the sweetest chuckle I've ever known. "Come on, Michael. You've been here before. It's time to get back on track."

Ten days later, most of the songs for an album called *One Heart in the Right Place* were written. When I quit worrying about myself and how to intensify the brilliance of that star on the rise, it was as if a flash flood of songs came pouring into my mind.

I've wondered why this happened the way it did, and why it came at that particular time in my creative life. What was it that triggered the deep inner questioning? Was it simply the way I dealt with the pressures I was facing, or was it more than that? Was it preparing me, somehow, to follow a different path than I would have otherwise chosen? For years I've felt that it could have been God's way of getting my attention and redirecting my creative energies in a way that would possibly benefit others. But what if it wasn't that at all? What if the only way I could overcome my deep insecurities and get something written and produced was to believe that my creative work was an important part of some heavenly design? If God needed me to help Him reach His children, then I could claim the ultimate shield to protect me from artistic criticism: that of being an instrument in the hands of the Almighty. At what point does a creative person who wants to use his gifts to do some good take responsibility for what may be lousy craft hiding behind lofty intentions? And where is the line drawn between hard work and talent and heavenly inspiration?

I don't know how it works for others, and I'm just starting to explore how it has worked for me, but here's what I think on the day I'm writing this down: I think I've tried to either blame or credit God with many things in my life that He'd probably appreciate me taking responsibility for myself. But that doesn't change my passionate belief that God knows us, and loves us, and has a plan remarkably tailored to help us figure out how to live happily. And for me, my happiest moments artistically and my most fulfilling moments creatively have come when I've acknowledged Him, *The Creator*, to be an essential part of my creative process. My nonbelieving friends might call this a crutch. I think of it more as a heavenly motorized wheelchair.

I've felt someone was listening when I've prayed for the patience to not be discouraged by a mediocre first draft, for the humility to listen to others and then plow through the second draft, for the insight to rewrite a better third draft, for the enthusiasm to face a fourth draft, for the tenacity to explore a fifth draft, for the courage to start all over again, and for the faith to trust whatever feels like the final draft. The thought that any of this would even matter to the One who governs the whole universe may seem absurdly arrogant to some, but it's deeply humbling to me. And that's why today I'm trying to be good, and doing what I'm doing for somebody besides myself.

CHAPTER 4

I Don't Understand

It was devastating. He'd been taken in his prime, leaving a wife and four children. I was asked to sing at the funeral.

She didn't look like a widow. She wasn't old enough, but she was. And as everyone lined up to express their deep sympathy before the casket was closed, I watched her comfort the mourners. It amazed me. She was comforting those who had come to comfort but didn't know how.

I barely got through my song. As much as I loved my missing friend, I looked at the faces of his wife and children and tried to imagine what their lives were going to be like after they were finished being strong for everyone else.

I wondered when that moment would come. It was during the World Series.

"Michael! Whatcha doin'?" Her voice sounded good, almost playful.

"Tryin' to get out of work. Got any really great excuses you think my wife'll buy?"

"Sure do. Tell her you have to rescue a widow and her father-less child."

"What's wrong?"

"It's sort of an emergency."

"Emergency?"

"Get here as soon as you can . . . and bring chocolate."

The smell of fresh popcorn was filling the front porch when I arrived. I could hear the national anthem coming from the TV in the den. The door opened before I knocked.

"Get in here. The game's about to begin."

Laid out on the coffee table in the den was the finest smorgasbord of baseball food I had ever seen: hot dogs, with kraut, onions, relish, and mustard in easy-scoop dishes; nachos with shredded beef, extra cheese, killer salsa, and jalapenos arranged in the shape of a baseball diamond; bean dip, cheddar dip, spinach-artichoke dip, pretzels, Cheetos, Corn Nuts, peanuts (in shells and out, candy coated and dry packed), and in every empty space on the table were dishes filled with Cracker Jacks and sunflower seeds, and some empty bowls I assumed were for the chocolate I was supposed to bring.

She took my chocolate offering from my hand. In the sack were some M&M's and a couple of Hershey's bars with almonds.

"This is it?" she said, looking at the paltry offering. "What are we gonna do if it goes extra innings?"

"If the game's close, I'll run to the market during the seventh-inning stretch," I offered.

Sitting on the couch, absorbed in an electronic handheld game, was her son.

"Hey, buddy, ready for the big game?" I asked.

He didn't look up. "I guess."

"Who we cheering for?"

He didn't answer. Maybe this was because he was battling aliens from another galaxy, and that can distract just about anyone, but I think the real reason he didn't answer was because he didn't care.

His mom pulled me into the kitchen.

"So, what's the big emergency I'm here for?"

"Could you just be a guy in the house for a couple of hours? Watch the game, yell at the umpires, eat too much and belch too loud and make a mess and act like it belongs there." Her eyes got a little moist. "There's too much estrogen in this house. I'm afraid he's gonna forget what guys are supposed to do when the Series is on."

We'd been friends for a long time, and I guess she knew she didn't have to be strong for me, so she broke down. That lasted about as long as a commercial break between innings. Then my friend performed a little ritual I suppose she'd done more than once. She pounded her fist against her thigh, shook her head, took a deep breath, and let it out slowly. "Why do people think it's comforting to tell a widow why they believe her husband had to die?" she asked.

"What do you mean?"

"Do you have any idea how many people have taken it upon themselves to tell me why my husband's gone? Somehow, they've been able to see beyond the veil and feel comforted in knowing that my husband was called home; that he had some special mission to perform on the other side; that God needed him. What's that? The Almighty can't get along without him, but the kids and I can? Do people even know what they're saying?"

"Probably not."

"Well then, why don't they just keep their mouths shut? Most of them don't have a clue what it's like, and yet somehow, through some spiritual gift only they possess, they understand all, see all, and know the mind and will of God and can tell me why our family has to suffer."

She wasn't looking for a response, so I didn't offer one.

"I'm sure everyone means well," she went on. "They don't know what to say but feel like they have to say something. Maybe the things they say are comforting to them, but they make me feel that much more alone. It seems that if anyone ought to be receiving an understanding about such a thing, it should be the one who's suffering. All I know for sure is that my husband is dead, and it doesn't seem right and it doesn't seem fair and it doesn't make any sense at all."

I wanted so much to make things better. My mind checked the index on human suffering and noted a lot of stuff—articles by C. S. Lewis, Psalms from David, and messages from prophets through the ages—all good stuff, powerful stuff, spiritually comforting stuff, but I got the feeling this wasn't the time or the place. It was time for dogs and suds, nachos and cheese, and handfuls of chocolate with Cracker-Jack chasers.

I can't remember who won the World Series. In fact, I can't remember who was playing that year. But I do remember the mess I made and the delight in my friend's eyes when I didn't even pretend to want to clean it up. Her son even put down his Game Boy long enough to join me in throwing popcorn at an ump who'd made a bad call.

When I got home, my heart was unsettled. Maybe I should have said something. I thought maybe I could sing things I couldn't say. Or, perhaps, the things she wasn't ready to hear in words, she could feel in melody. I wanted to write a song that could express some of those profound spiritual truths that have been given as gifts from gospel scholars, spiritual giants, and ancient holy men, but that song didn't get written that day. Instead, one that said this did:

> It would be crazy for me to even try to pretend
> That I know what you're going through,
> And I haven't found answers that make sense to me,
> So I don't have an answer for you. . . .
> And I don't understand,
> So I'm not sure
> How to help you get through.
> I'm just hoping that you will see
> That I'm saying that I care,
> That I always will be here,
> And that I understand one thing eternally—
> And that's how much you'll always mean to me.

33

CHAPTER 5

THE ONE AND ONLY YOU

I picked thirty-five. Could have been forty, could have been later, but for some reason I thought that by the time I reached the age of thirty-five, maturity would start manifesting itself in my life. I thought I'd feel kind of grown-up by then, and start speaking and acting like the grown-ups I had always respected in my life.

There was a look on the faces of mature people that I wondered why I'd never seen on my own face. It was a confident, quietly self-assured look, not easily rattled, friendly, but filled with wisdom: a cross between Ward Cleaver, my dad, a local television news anchor, and my friend Gary Jubber.

I'd been in several meetings with mature people, and I noticed the way they interacted with other community leaders; the way they commented on matters of business, politics, and church; the way they carried themselves in general. Not one, not even *one* (as far as I could see) ever jumped out of his chair in the midst of a discussion and yelled, "Are you kidding me? This is nuts! What planet are you guys living on?" And I never saw any of them get so emotional or passionate in a presentation that tears came to their eyes. No siree. These were mature people, and I admired them because the world was stable and safe in their hands.

By the time I turned thirty-five, the feeling of being settled down and settled in, which I hoped would just happen, hadn't. As I approached forty there was still no real evidence that I was *ever* going to act and feel like a grown-up. Oh, I had a mortgage, three kids, and a wife to whom I had stayed married since I was twenty-two, but that didn't count. I didn't feel much different from how I had felt at eighteen. So one day I decided to change.

My first step to becoming mature was to declutter my office. All the posters, pictures, sticky notes, T-shirts from rock concerts, enlarged cartoons from the Far Side, all of it—gone. I went through my file cabinets and threw away stuff that wasn't worthy of my new status as a grown-up person. I rearranged the furniture so that it looked like somebody old enough to actually have a job at a company worked in that office.

I started dressing differently as well. Suits and ties instead of sweaters, slacks instead of jeans, Sunday shoes replaced the Reeboks, and I wore shirts that somebody at the dry cleaning place had starched.

Of course I had to have a voice that matched the new look, so I worked on speaking a bit like the men who broadcast the news—not the network guys, but the local guys. (I had to start realistically.) I quit jumping up in meetings, screaming, "I got it, I got it!"

and then presenting whatever idea had popped into my head as if it had come directly from God's mouth to my ear. I started holding back. Started saying things like, "I'll have to think about that," before responding. I nodded my head a lot, to show that I was thinking deeply about what was taking place around me, and I completely stopped, cold turkey, telling people how excited I felt about something I'd just written.

I had sustained this newly found pose for about a month—it might have been as long as five weeks—before I accidentally slid off the maturity wagon.

I was driving to work in my little Datsun 240Z, a very used sports car I had gotten as payment for a commercial I'd done for a car dealership years before. On the way, I decided it was time to change the preset buttons on the radio to include more "appropriate" stations. In the process, I pushed the button of a previously beloved rock station just as the Boss was singing "Darlington County" from the *Born in the U.S.A.* album. At that moment, alone in the car, it seemed almost sacrilegious for me, having graduated from high school in New Jersey, not to crank it up and sing along with Bruce Springsteen, the coolest rockin' daddy in the U.S.A.

Not only did I crank the radio up loud enough so that it bounced the shocks in my car, but I sang along with the reckless abandon of a teenager on his first solo drive in a hot set of wheels.

When a traffic light forced me to stop at the corner of Seventh East and Ninth South, I took advantage of this opportunity to use the steering wheel as a drum set and I pounded away. Out of the corner of my eye I could see, sitting in a Lexus right next to me, a true grown-up. The look was unmistakable. He observed me, over the top of his grown-up guy glasses, with a mixture of condescending amusement and disdain that crushed my mood like a power outage at a battle of the bands. I'd been found out. I was embarrassed and immediately turned the radio down and sat up straight and regained a mature, upright position. Unfortunately, when I straightened up, my foot slipped off the clutch, and I sort of herky-jerked my way through the intersection.

For the next few blocks I beat myself up for being such an idiot. It wasn't because the guy in the fancy car disapproved; I didn't even know who he was. It was because I wasn't making the transition into the grown-up world very well. Singing at the top of my lungs with the windows rolled down and the Boss rattling the speakers of my go-fast wasn't in keeping with the man I was trying to be—the respected, got-it-all-together, trusted friend and ally who deserved the title Mister (with a capital M) McLean. I was disappointed that my makeover on the outside hadn't affected the real me inside.

And then I felt as if something were sweetly wrapping itself around my soul. That's the only way I can describe it. It was warm and tender and felt like liquid understanding flowing from my head to my heart. And I wondered why I had turned the radio down. For the next few moments, deep in thought, I imagined a conversation with the most mature Being in all the universe sitting next to me in that car.

"I like Bruce too."

I started to laugh and cry at the same moment. It was such an extraordinary and surprising thing to imagine: God, telling me how much He liked Bruce Springsteen. But that was nothing compared to the thoughts that followed:

"Look, I know how hard you're trying to be this grown-up guy, and I completely understand. But you're going about it all wrong. To tell you the truth, I've been missing the old Michael. I really, really liked you the way you were. You see, I made only one of you—just one—and if you run so far away from that guy that even I don't recognize you, something very special in the universe is lost."

I pulled over to the side of the road. I didn't want to get to work too soon; this was way too wonderful to miss.

"Wanting to be better is a good thing. Reaching higher, setting standards, growing and becoming are all important goals. But don't waste your energy working on a bad impersonation of somebody else. Work on being the best *you* that you can be."

I started the car back up. Two blocks before I got to the office, I loosened my tie, and it felt so good that I took it off.

I could breathe again.

> *There is a place here that only you can fill,*
> *And this empty space awaits the magic you instill,*
> *For your warm embrace does what nothing else can do:*
> *You're second to none because you're the one and only you.*

CHAPTER 6

It Wasn't Love Before

They weren't what you'd call a "churchy" couple, but they wore their own special religion like a comfortable pair of jeans—nothing fancy, yet very practical and nearly impossible to wear out.

Although they didn't come to church much, anyone who knew them wasn't all that worried about their immortal souls. That may have been because Bonnie would do anything for you or anyone at any time you needed it . . . and she'd make you feel like you were doing her a favor if you let her. She was just good, and you felt it when you were around her. Nobody knew that goodness more than Carl.

It must have been twenty years that Carl's legs didn't work. But that didn't mean he didn't get around. Bonnie made sure of that. Wherever he was, whether it was on a tractor or in a car running errands or puttering around somewhere on their farm, Bonnie made sure her Carl got there with full dignity intact. Maybe that was why such a big part of her tiny little frame felt so empty when Carl passed away. In her case, it was more literal than figurative: Part of her was missing.

Sadly, that emptiness filled with cancer. It wasn't clear whether she had chosen to fight it with a passion Spartacus would envy or just to ignore it like a yoga master at a meditation retreat. It's unbelievable how tough this woman was. With full-on cancer, she insisted on moving her own sprinkler pipes. It was as if she found her own unique treatment in the form of a game: If she personally got her crops to grow faster than the cancer, she would win.

Well, she wasn't winning the day I visited her in the hospital and the pain was so overwhelming she begged for a morphine shot. Seeing her in that hospital bed, curled up in a fetal position and weeping in pain, I didn't think she would see another Sunday. The most compassionate part of me hoped she wouldn't have to.

But she rallied. She survived an operation to remove some obstruction and greeted me the next Sunday with her trademark smile. "They won't let me eat anything yet," she mourned, "and I'm so hungry I could eat the north end of a southbound skunk."

She was back. Classic Bonnie, trying to figure out how to get home sooner and take care of her animals. We chatted a while. I hadn't known her that well for that long—most of what I knew about her, I learned from lifelong friends who adored her—so I asked her to tell me a little bit about Carl. It was as if you had asked a teenager to talk about her first love. She was proud and shy at the same time. She wanted me to understand just how wonderful he was, and how much she missed him.

"When I got sick, about a year before he died, he stopped eating," she said. Her eyes showed just a hint of tears—not so much that he'd be embarrassed if he were listening, but enough to let me know she was telling her most precious truth.

"He barely ate enough to stay alive. When I got well enough to help him around again, he was nothing but heart and bones. I said, 'Carl, we've gotta get some meat on you, you're practically wasting away . . .'"

She paused. Perhaps she wondered if what she was about to say was too private or too sacred to share with someone outside the family's innermost circle. I don't know why, but I'm grateful she carried on.

"Then he told me, 'I thought I'd be a little easier to lift if I didn't eat so much.'"

Bonnie didn't say anything else about her relationship with Carl. She didn't have to.

> It wasn't that I lied, all those times I said I love you—
> I really loved you.
> I meant it when I said before I couldn't love you anymore.
> It wasn't that I lied, but time has brought new meaning to
> This "I love you,"
> And compared to how I love you now,
> It's almost like it wasn't love before.

CHAPTER 7

CELEBRATING THE LIGHT

In 1989 I wrote a musical review called *Celebrating the Light*, and it ran for five summer seasons at a beautiful little theater called the Promised Valley Playhouse. There were probably a lot of reasons the show ran as long as it did: The cast was a terrific group of college entertainers who had their own following and had been inspiring crowds around the world for decades. The community had a tradition of attending this theater that dated back half a century. The production value for the show was remarkable, given the ticket price, and so it felt like an amazing "deal" for live theater. And because it was subsidized, the show was cheaper than a movie. Ask anyone who's been there and they'll tell you, it was an absolutely charming space, and in the heat of the summer, the air conditioning was great.

Of course, I thought the show was a hit because of me.

The line between ego and ignorance has often been very blurry for me—obviously—but I believed there was something magic about that show that must have been inspiration or else the crowds wouldn't have lined up to see it summer after summer after summer.

With more naivete than arrogance, I told my wife that I thought we needed to take the show out on the road. I explained to her how we would hire a terrific group of college-age entertainers, offer the show at extremely affordable prices so families could come, and go to places where we knew some folks who liked my music.

"How you planning on financing this, Michael?"

"Well, I guess we could go out and look for investors, but I just hate asking people for money. Maybe we should take some savings and invest in ourselves and do some good with it."

"How much of our savings do you think it'll take?" A fair question coming from my partner in life, my dearest companion, and the one who handled most of the money anyway.

"How much have we got?" I asked.

She told me.

"That ought to about do it. And won't we feel better about using our money for something that matters, rather than just having it sit around earning interest?" I said this as if it made perfect sense.

"So," she responded, "you want to take everything we have and finance a traveling production of *Celebrating the Light*. You think you should charge only eight or ten dollars a ticket because otherwise families won't be able to afford to go."

As she was patiently reviewing what she understood to be my great plan for our life savings, I imagined her ending it all with the thought: "*Are you crazy? If nobody comes, we won't be able to* afford to go to *any* show at *any* price." But she didn't. She listened as I tried to explain that we were going to hire somebody to do advertising, and that we just had to have a little faith in ourselves. Life was about taking risks, blah blah blah; we may not make a lot of money, but we would surely recoup our investment, blah blah blah; and we would probably do a lot of good along the way.

She listened to the dream, as she had for so many years, and smiled the way she always did when she was about to give me her support. "Do you need it all at once, or in chunks?"

After four shows of a thirty-five-show tour, I knew we were in trouble. Even on the nights we had decent crowds, we were losing money. By the second week we were hemorrhaging money so fast no tourniquet could stop it. Some nights there were almost more people on stage than in the audience.

I went through all the stages of loss and grief about every forty-five minutes of every day. How could this have happened? I wanted to blame the promotional guy, or the advertising team, or the fans who wouldn't support me, or anyone who came to mind, but the truth was, it was my fault. I had gone into this adventure without enough preparation on the business end, and with way too much faith without works.

Don't get me wrong. It wasn't all gloom and doom. The good news was that the show itself was wonderful, and most towns had cheap pizza that could be paid for on any given night if we sold ten CDs, five T-shirts, and a couple of hats.

By the time we got to Seattle, I realized that I'd lost everything. Even if the rest of the shows on the tour sold well, it was over. It would take years and years to recover, if I ever did. I wasn't handling it well. I could tell because I was using expressions I used to think were defensible only if you'd smashed your thumb with a hammer. And I was crying a lot.

That evening we had booked two shows, and I was in a local bookstore trying to sell a few more tickets and schlep a couple of CDs. I was hoping that if we were lucky, we might be able to avoid contracting scurvy and actually have a green salad added to our after-show meal.

It was about three in the afternoon and the store was virtually empty when a woman and her three children came in. The mother spotted me instantly and walked toward me with the sweetness of a long-lost relative.

"Michael, you're here! I was afraid we wouldn't make it in time. I've come to get tickets for the show tonight."

"Thank you so much," I said. "You have no idea how much this means to me."

She asked me if I would sign the back of the tickets she purchased, and as I did, I asked her about the large patch over her eye.

"What happened to your eye?" I avoided staring by focusing on my autographs.

"Oh, my eye—not there anymore."

"What happened?"

"Too many surgeries. They went through the eye socket to get to the tumor, and after the last couple of trips to the operating room it never worked quite right, so the doctors and I decided to leave it out."

You know, you can keep your eyes on the signing of a ticket for only so long, and then you sort of have to look up. Having heard what she told me, I feared I was going to look at her the way my third-grade teacher had told me not to look at someone in a wheelchair.

I tried to disguise my real reactions by saying something upbeat. "Well, the surgeries must have been successful because you're here and you look great."

"Well, all but this last one was. Turns out they couldn't get all of the tumor, and it's malignant and it's fatal." She didn't say this the way I thought someone with an inoperable brain tumor would share such information. She wasn't depressed, she wasn't self-pitying, she wasn't playing the noble heroine. She just said it like it was.

I noticed that her children, whom I guessed to be about eight, five, and maybe three years old, were at the other end of the store, so I asked her quietly, "How long do you have?"

"You know, Michael, either they don't know or they just won't tell me. But I think I'll make it through tonight, so don't mess up."

She laughed a big laugh and patted me on the back in a way that let me know I didn't need to be self-conscious about what had been said because she certainly wasn't.

That night the shows went well. After the second one, my friend with the patch on her eye came running up to me in the foyer where I was signing the back of a T-shirt. She wasn't trying to be rude, but she couldn't wait to get to the front of the line, and when I saw her I accommodated. She was the kind of woman you just knew you could hug, and so I did. She was crying.

"Michael, Michael, Michael. Do you have any idea what you

have given me tonight? I have worried about what I could give my children that they could hang onto when I was gone. And tonight, with this show, was the gift with a message I prayed I could give them, so thank you, thank you, thank you! Our family will treasure this for a long, long time. Bless you, bless you. You'll never know . . . you'll never know."

After the show, the tour manager asked me if I had any idea how much we'd made that night. For me, at that moment, the answer was: twice what I dreamed of, and more than I deserved. The title song of the show we were touring took on new meaning.

> *I believe there's a light that shines in everyone—*
> *I believe it's the Light of the World.*
> *I believe there's a voice that whispers there's a choice,*
> *And our joy will come from choosing what is right*
> *And celebrating the light.*

On the way to Boise the next day, I told the tour manager we ought to stop for lunch at someplace nice. You know, with steaks and a real nice salad bar.

"You know what that's gonna cost."

Doesn't matter, I thought. *We've got something to celebrate.*

But the "celebration" was short-lived. I wish the impact of that woman's story could have fully sustained me through the financial disaster of the tour, but it didn't. There's something about losing money (big chunks of your own hard-earned cash) that finds its way to center stage even when you've tried to write it out of the script.

I would call home with updates on how things were going and try to apologize to Lynne for losing all our money. Because I was so distraught about the financial situation, I was convinced my wife was too, but she seemed to be more worried about me, what this was doing to my spirit, how this was affecting my faith in myself and in my ability to follow the light I was singing about every night. While I ended each day praying for a miracle, she was praying for *me*.

The miracle of big crowds, massive CD sales, financial resuscitation, and corporate sponsorships never materialized, but that doesn't mean a miracle didn't happen. The miracle was my wife. She kept praying for me by night and cheering me on by day. Those calls, and her surprise visits during some of the most difficult parts of the tour, were my connection with what really mattered. Not only did she support me throughout the entire ordeal but she never criticized me for what I'd chosen to do with our money and my time. She never criticized me for losing my perspective, or for having such a hard time letting go. She listened, she understood, she didn't run away emotionally or physically. She loved me in a way I never knew I could be loved, and I didn't fully appreciate it until long after the crisis ended.

I've often said that she is the reason my heart has a song, but there are lyrics to the song "Celebrating the Light" that I now know belong more to her than I ever realized.

> *Celebrating the light, that shines in one and all*
> *And lifts us when we fall,*
> *And answers when we call.*

CHAPTER 8

LET IT GO

𝄞

I was broke. How broke? Make-your-own-pizza-and-watch-PBS broke. I'd lost all our savings on that little venture I mentioned in the last chapter, and although I felt we had done some good, with each passing day and each arriving bill I was less impressed with what we had accomplished. I believed I was the guy who actually had *STUPID* written on my forehead.

It was the end of summer, and there was a convention for all the wholesalers and retailers who sold my books and music. Given my situation, I attacked the convention like a used-car salesman during a summer Sale-a-Bration. I was a bit much, which surprised no one who knew me. With the holiday season approaching, I was pushing a Christmas-story-with-music package I'd written called *The Forgotten Carols.* As a special inducement to order big, I told the merchants that for every copy they bought, a sin would be removed.

The booth where I was working was right next to one that housed Richard Paul Evans, the author of a little book called *The Christmas Box*. He was signing autographs and celebrating the news that some big-time publisher had bought rights to his book for *millions* of dollars. Oh, and in a few months his story would be seen on network television starring John-Boy Walton (I know he's got a real name, but he'll always be John-Boy to me) and Maureen O'Hara. *Maureen O'Hara!* The woman who made me wish I was John Wayne.

Richard was nursing a cold that day, but he was as kind and gracious as could be, and it seemed to me that I ought to congratulate him on his success. I approached the booth to do this very magnanimous thing that would go down in the history of the world as one of the six most humble and thoughtful acts ever performed by someone not named Gandhi. *And I had to stand in line!*

The longer I waited, the harder it was to keep that plastic smile on my face. This guy was a *millionaire* who was probably going to have lunch with Maureen O'Hara, and I had to stand in line to pay homage at the altar of his phenomenal luck. Oh, the injustice, the horror.

When I finally got my audience with Mr. Evans, I gave my little congratulatory speech, which would have come across much more sincerely if I had written it down and mailed it to him because he wouldn't have noticed that the words were coming from a man who'd turned *green*.

All the way home I kept thinking how totally unfair the universe was. I mean, come on, if there were any book that ought to make millions of dollars, it was *mine*. My book wasn't just a touching little sentimental Christmas story. It was a touching little sentimental Christmas story *with songs*. I didn't see Richard Paul Evans writing any songs for his book.

And if there were any justice in the world, shouldn't the guy who had slaved for seventeen years at a production company learning how to make movies be the one to take Ms. O'Hara to the prom?

I said none of these things out loud, of course, to anyone. But I couldn't hide what I was feeling from myself. There was a continuous tape loop of the injustice that played over and over and over in my head and, try as I might, I couldn't switch it off.

As a kid, I had learned that sometimes if you wanted to feel a certain way, you had to act a certain way, and the feelings would follow. I tried acting like I was excited for someone else's success and not miserable about my own failure, but it didn't work. The harder I tried, the worse it got, because I became more convinced that the heavens had shafted me.

This led to a very painful discovery. It's exhausting being a jealous creep on the inside while masquerading as a really wonderful guy on the outside. It occurred to me that the kind of people I always wanted to be invited to lunch with weren't searching the black market for voodoo dolls of millionaire authors. I began a self-examination that took me deep into the recesses of my soul, and I found a couple of other things down there that I wasn't too proud of.

So I made a list of all the things that I noticed weren't so wonderful about me, and it was six pages long. *Six pages!* And then I thought of a few more things about myself that needed to change. I was overwhelmed.

I went to the top of the list, where I'd written about my issues of jealousy and envy in great detail, and put them in a separate file labeled: *Things I just can't do by myself.* I then told God how sorry I was that I kind of hated one of His children and couldn't manufacture an even slightly sincere feeling of happiness for him no matter how hard I tried. I also told the Almighty that I wasn't turning this over to Him because I thought He'd be mad at me for not getting this fixed on my own, but because I just hated the way I felt inside and didn't want to carry it any longer. For all my phoniness and pretending with others, my little prayer was actually sincere.

The heavens didn't open. I heard no voices. There was silence.

Because I didn't know what else to do, I just left it alone for a while, there in the separate file. I let it go.

About six weeks later, I was shopping alone in Sam's Club, and I came upon this massive display of a new book by Colin Powell, who had received so much attention for his role in the first Gulf War. It was an impressive display, to say the least, and right next to it, even more impressive, was a banner that read: "The Most Successful Christmas Story Since *A Christmas Carol:* Richard Paul Evans' *The Christmas Box.*"

It was an amazing sight. There is no writer on the face of the earth who wouldn't weep for joy at such a promotion for his or her work. It was gorgeous and classy and just beyond wonderful.

And as I looked at it, I heard myself say, "Way to go, Richard."

I meant it. I felt it. It was real. I couldn't believe it. Genuine, true feelings were filling me up. I was so happy for this guy. It stunned me how this was happening, and I started to cry in the aisle at Sam's Club. And it wasn't just wipe-your-eye crying. It was shake-your-shoulders, face-in-your-hands, goobers-in-the-nose crying.

People would gently approach me and ask if I was okay.

"Isn't it a beautiful display?" was all I could say.

You know, there are little miracles that happen all the time—like Moses parting the Red Sea—and then every once in a while God does something *really* impossible just to remind us that He's God. He changes somebody's heart.

> *All that's wrong in your life, let it go.*
> *All that is worth saving is love—*
> *Love will hold you tight.*
> *Love lifts the burden and love shines the light.*
> *Only love nourishes us so;*
> *If it's not love,*
> *Simply let it go.*

CHAPTER 9

LET HIM IN

I thought it was an obvious question, so I asked it. "Who wants or needs new Christmas songs? We've already got 'White Christmas,' 'Chestnuts Roasting,' 'Silent Night,' and Handel's *Messiah.*"

This was my best argument for *not* doing a Christmas album. My record label countered, "But look at the huge success of Mannheim Steamroller's Christmas albums."

"Those records aren't collections of new songs, they're new arrangements of old ones, and they prove my point, which is that at Christmas we hunger for tradition; we crave the familiar. How else do you explain eggnog and fruitcake? And who would be arrogant enough to think they could write original material that would belong in the same CD player as the greatest and most beloved music of all time?"

Why were they looking at me like that? I didn't know whether their silence was a form of agreement or an indictment. They asked me to just think about it again.

"I already have, since you asked me last year, and the answer's the same. I just don't have anything to bring to the party. Sorry."

A part of me really wished I were a clever arranger or a wonderful orchestrator so that I *could* do what they wanted, but I was a storytelling songwriter out of his depth when it came to Christmas.

I thought about it a lot, though. Wondered what musical approach to Christmas might cause me to reexamine and deepen my own feelings for the holiday. And then I would put on my favorite Christmas albums and realize that it had already been done by masters.

I can't remember what sparked the idea (perhaps it was a couple of years of wondering about it subconsciously), but early one December evening I was sitting at the piano and a thought popped into my heart, along with a glimpse of a melody. What if we got a chance to talk to the innkeeper who turned away Joseph and Mary? What would he tell us? Maybe something like: "I am a man forgotten and no one recalls my name. Thousands of years have failed to fully erase my shame."

There's a moment in the creative process when something comes out of the blue, like a gift from a cherished but distant friend, that is so exciting it surpasses the thrill of your first bicycle. You can't quite believe you're so lucky, and you can't wait to learn how to ride it.

As I was trying to channel the innkeeper and transcribe his

thoughts onto my legal-size yellow pad, my son leaned against the doorjamb at the entrance to my writing room and just stood there.

"What's up?" I said, without giving him too much eye contact.

"Nothin'."

"You need something?" I said while penciling in a list of words that rhymed with *shame*.

"Nah . . ." He shuffled his feet, looked down, and put his hands in his pockets.

For anyone who's ever had a twelve-year-old, the grunts, shrugs, monosyllables, and shuffling are all part of a code language that isn't all that difficult to translate, if you're not in the middle of writing a song.

"You wanna talk about something?" I kept looking at the yellow pad and repeated a riff on the piano a few times. But I wasn't completely insensitive. I played it softly.

My son shifted his weight and mumbled something that sounded like "I'm okay."

"Good. Well if there's anything you need, let me know . . ." I offered a partial glance, but no real eye contact. That might have distracted me and chased away the elusive creative muse that had just distilled upon my soul after years in hibernation.

I can't recall exactly how long he stood there in the doorjamb. I was too busy working on the song that might change the world. After all, wasn't this my special gift? Didn't I have a responsibility to develop my talents (not to mention pay the light bill)? More than enough justification for me. I spent the next couple of hours finishing the song.

When I get really excited about a new song, I often sit at the piano in the middle of the night and play it over and over again until it feels pretty good to me. Then I start searching for an audience. Whoever's in the house gets rounded up first. Sometimes, if nobody's home and I'm desperate for feedback, I'll start calling friends and singing the latest creation over the phone. I'm not shy about grabbing people at the office or at church and strong-arming them to the nearest piano for a little private concert. I don't believe I sought my son's opinion of this song. Strange, isn't it, since the words that I thought were about the innkeeper and the babe of Bethlehem were really about myself and my son.

I am a man forgotten; no one recalls my name.
Thousands of years will fail to fully erase my shame.
But I turned a profit nicely that day
That I turned the couple away—
I turned them away.

I didn't sleep that evening, though I'd sold out my place.
Somehow I felt uneasy . . . something about her face.
Why do I wish that I'd let them stay?
I didn't think they could pay . . . or could they have paid?

Restless I left my bedroom—I walked the streets all night,
Lost in the world I lived in,
Found by a heavenly light.
Staring at one bright star in the sky,
I heard a baby cry.

And I knew where the cry had come from,
'Cause I'd told them where they could go,
But I didn't think I could face them
So I walked slowly home,
Missing my chance to share in their joy—
I never saw the boy.

He never would condemn me;
I did that all on my own.
He offered His forgiveness,
And ever since then I've known
He lets us choose each hour of each day
If we'll let Him in to stay.

Let Him in . . . let Him in . . .
Let the joy and hope begin.
Let Him in . . . let Him in . . .
Let the peace on earth begin.
And whether it be in your world today
Or a crowded Bethlehem inn,
Find a way, make Him room,
Let Him in.

My enthusiasm for the new Christmas song (and the album and book that followed) prevented me for quite some time, I'm ashamed to say, from seeing its deeper meaning. And my apology to my son was postponed far too long because I was so distracted by the attention given my newly born song-child.

I'm afraid that early in my career my song-children often received more attention than my flesh-and-blood children, possibly because I could mold my musical offspring just to my liking and they never complained. They did what they were told and became what I wanted them to become, and I could hold them up to the world and take credit for them.

Human beings are a different deal. You can try to shape them and mold them, but in the end, they get to choose who and how they want to be. And the credit for their success belongs to them.

As much as my songs have taught me, I never brought a song into the world that taught me as much as my unique, independent, creative, spontaneous, insightful, passionate, intense children. Come to think of it, it's their musical siblings (like "Let Him In") that have tried to teach me where my greatest happiness would be found, and from whom my greatest lessons would be learned. How this all works, and works so well, is a mystery, a miracle, and a gift . . . like Christmas itself.

CHAPTER 10

IT'S NICE WHEN SOME
THINGS ARE FORGOTTEN

In 1976 I was hired to be the producer of the radio and television broadcasts of the Mormon Tabernacle Choir. The primary responsibility was the weekly broadcast of *Music and the Spoken Word,* which is to this day the longest continuously running network radio broadcast in the world. The format of this remarkably successful program had been defined and refined for decades before I was born—so, naturally, upon being hired as the show's newest producer, I tried to change it.

Maybe we could try this? Wouldn't it be more moving if we did that? Don't you think the audience would love it if we . . . and so on. I remember suggesting in a meeting once that to broaden the appeal of the already world-famous choir, we should get them a guest spot on *The Muppet Show.* There must have been something about the prospect of Miss Piggy or Gonzo popping out of the

Tabernacle organ pipes that brought that noticeable chill into the room.

Fortunately, in my nearly five-year tenure as the producer of the Choir's broadcasts, I failed to make a single change in the format of *Music and the Spoken Word,* other than my constant request that the Choir members all "beam" more.

Of the many, many wonderful people I got to know and work with during those years, there was one woman for whom I had a particular fascination: Marianne Fisher, the first blind woman to be a member of the Choir. She amazed me. I'm sure she amazed everyone who watched her closely enough to discover what she had trained herself to do, yet I always had the distinct impression that she didn't want to draw that much attention to herself.

For those of you who never had the privilege of knowing her, I'd like to let you see a remarkable woman through my eyes.

"Michael, dear, if you really want them to imagine me, have 'em close their eyes."

"But Marianne, if they close their eyes, they won't be able to read what I've written."

"What's the matter with 'em? Are they handicapped?"

Dear readers: Meet my friend Marianne Fisher.

"Hi. I usually get my hair right, but it's the rouge that's really hard. Is it even? Did I blend it right? Now come on, tell me the truth. I don't want you to be uncomfortable. I mean, nobody wants to hurt a blind woman's feelings, but I really need to know. It's one of the frustrations of being blind . . . as independent as I've tried to become, there are just some things you can't do without help.

"There. Did I get it? If you're feeling a little awkward right now because I'm disabled, you really shouldn't make that big a deal out of it. I mean, as far as I can tell, *everybody* is disabled in some way. There are just some things we're all unable to do by ourselves, no matter how hard we try. If you don't believe me, consider this: Are you a singer? Yes. Well, try being a choir by yourself. I rest my case.

"I was the first blind woman to be made a member of the Mormon Tabernacle Choir. For years and years my dream of singing with the Choir was placed on the back, back burner until a wonderful conductor named Jerold Ottley gave me an opportunity to audition.

"You know, it's a funny thing, really. Singers spend so much of their lives developing their talents so they'll stand out and be noticed, and yet to sing in a great choir you have to show you can blend in. Well, being blind in a sighted world is a bit like being a green grape in a bowl of cherries; you just can't help but stick out somehow. Anyway, there I was, going to the audition, trying desperately hard to prove that I could blend in.

"I had another reason I wanted to be in the Choir: my father. My father loved the Tabernacle Choir—he rarely had anything good to say about the Mormon church, but he loved the Choir. After his problem with alcohol became more than my mother could bear, they were divorced. We kept in touch, but there were rough spots, to be sure. But even though there were many heartaches in that relationship, one of the things we did share was our love for that wonderful Choir. Daddy passed away in 1969, seven years before my big audition.

"As I took the tests and performed the songs, I kept hoping they'd forget I was blind and just listen to my voice and my heart as I sang."

Humbly I stood trembling in my shoes,
Hoping they'd hear I had paid my dues,
And as I sang, in my heart and mind
I prayed that justice was truly blind.
And when my singing was over, waiting patiently,
He said while listening to me that he forgot I could not see . . .
It's nice when some things are forgotten.

"You know, I was later told that on the test to get into the Choir I got 99 out of 100. I'm kind of glad I missed one. If I had been perfect, somebody may have thought I was looking off someone else's paper.

"I'll never forget that first time when I sat with the Choir and sang the opening strains of the theme for their Sunday morning broadcast. I wanted so much to cry, but I held it in. The cameras may have caught me crying, and somebody watching may have worried that something was wrong. I didn't want to do anything that would distract the audience from the message of our music."

I took my place 'midst that heavenly choir,
Hoping my flame added to their great fire.
Even though blind I could clearly see
Some weren't quite sure how to be with me,

But music bound us together in sweet harmony—
And as we sang in unity, they saw no disability.
It's nice when some things are forgotten.
And every time I join the choir to sing,
I feel my father watching in the wings.
And in some miracle from up above,
The only memory I have is love.

"I made my peace with my father singing in the Tabernacle Choir. There was such forgiveness and understanding and love as I sang. I'm not sure I understand how that happened, but it did. Maybe there's something in the music we're able to sing in that choir that helps children make peace with their Father, if they're only willing."

Someday, I pray, when my life is sung,
I'll be in tune with the Holy One.
And when He asks how my life has been,
I hope I proved that I could blend in.
And when the pain of remembering all my sins rushes in,
And I turn away from Him,
He'll tell me that He paid the debt and all my sins He did forget.
When He forgives, all is forgotten—
It's nice when some things are forgotten.

CHAPTER 11

WHICH PART IS MINE?

She was only a dairyman's daughter.
She was only a child of thirteen,
And the stars on the radio brightened her nights with a dream.
So she called up her best girlfriend, Jenny,
'Cause she thought they would make quite a pair.
She said, "Let's you and me try to sing harmony
At the amateur night at the fair."
But she only had the range of an alto,
So the part she knew best went to her friend.
And when Jenny's soprano drowned out the piano
They'd have to start over again.
And the dairyman's daughter would then say,
"Which part is mine, and which part is yours?
Could you tell me one more time; I'm never quite sure.
And I won't cross the line like I have before,

If you'll just tell me which part is mine
And which part is yours."

Well, she grew up and got married to Bobby
And kept him working on his MBA.
They had two little red-headed children and one on the way.
Everybody said she could work wonders,
And she wondered what everyone meant.
She played so many roles it was taking its toll
And she feared that her life was misspent.
So she opened her heart to her husband.
They discussed everything on her list
From the kids to her job to her feelings for Bob,
But it really just boiled down to this . . . she said,
"Which part is mine, and Bob, which part is yours?
Let's review this one more time, 'cause I'm never quite sure.
And I won't cross the line like I have before
If we'll just review which part is mine, and which part is yours."

Every sleepless night knows many mothers
Who are wondering if they've done all right.
And the dairyman's daughter knew more than a few of those nights.
Had she given her son too much freedom?
Had she smothered her two teenage girls?
Did she spoil them too much or not trust them enough
To prepare them for life in this world?
So she opened her heart to the heavens
And she spoke of her children by name.

And the prayer that she prayed that her kids would be saved
Had a very familiar refrain. She said,
"Which part is mine, and God, which part is yours?
Could you tell me one more time, 'cause I'm never quite sure.
And I won't cross the line like I have before,
But it gets so confusing sometimes.
Should I do more or trust the Divine?
Could you please tell me which part is mine and which part is yours?"

When I first wrote the song, that was where it ended. I played it for my wife, who said, "That's not the ending, is it?"

"Yes, it is."

"Michael, it can't be. It's too depressing."

"Depressing? It's not depressing, it's life. Can't you see, I have captured a truth about life in my song. Every day, when we wake up, we have to decide how much is up to us and how much we can turn over to someone or something else. Is today the day that if it's meant to be it's up to me, or is today the day to just let go and let God?"

I was on a roll. I think that if you listened closely you could have heard a church organ underscore my little sermonette.

"Is today the day that when the going gets tough, the tough get going?" I went on. "Or is it a day when you trust that you've done all you can do and show some faith? Can't you see, Lynne, this song, perhaps more than any other song I've written, has captured a truth about life."

"Yeah, in a really depressing way. Can't you fix the ending?"

We'd been married a long time, and I had learned not to get defensive when my wife offered constructive criticism of my songs. So I listened, actively, and when the mood seemed right, I said, "*So how many songs have YOU ever written?*"

"Good-night, Michael. Play me that song again sometime, when it's finished."

I was *not* going to change that song. The artist in me was not going to compromise just to make Pollyanna happy. You know, I never discussed this with her, but I think my wife truly believed Romeo and Juliet should have lived.

I was too riled up to sleep, so I went to the "great room" of our house. Perhaps I should mention here that at that time our place was sort of like *The Waltons* television show, and I was John-Boy. My mom and dad lived there, along with my wife and our three kids, as well as my sister and her husband and their three children. The central gathering place of the house we called the "great room." It had a wonderful piano in it, and with the logs and rock and high ceiling it sounded great.

I played through the song again, imagining how it would sound, unchanged, recorded in a professional studio with terrific players and a great singer.

I got to the final few lines: "It gets so confusing sometimes. Should I do more or trust the Divine? Could you please tell me which part is mine and which part is yours . . ." But when I came to the word *yours*, I accidentally hit the wrong chord, creating an almost eerie texture to the song. As the harmonics rang through the room and put the context of the song into an entirely different key,

I saw in my mind's eye the dairyman's daughter I'd been singing about. She was in her kitchen, grating carrots. Then she dropped everything into the sink and leaned against the counter with her head bowed and her fingers interlaced.

And I heard her sing:

Did you hear me?

It was so faint I almost missed it.

I can feel you near me . . .

I could see her lower lip tremble.

This is the answer that I've been longing for:
Just to know you hear me
And to feel you near me.
This is the answer
That I've been longing for.

I could hear violins swelling and the woodwinds echoing. It was so beautiful I couldn't stop, and strangely, I knew how she was feeling. Living under the same roof with so many family members (nuclear and extended) all needing so much attention, understanding, and love, and not knowing if and/or when you've done enough can really make you yearn for answers to life's big questions, like, "Which part is mine, and which part is yours?" Yet when you've been struggling for a long time, wondering if anyone up there knows what you're going through, and then you feel that closeness, it's so healing you don't ever want it to leave. It's curious to me that what often brings the comfort is not a specific answer to a question, but *knowing* you are actually being heard.

Yes, I knew how my dairyman's daughter felt, and so I joined her, loudly, in the refrain:

DO YOU HEAR ME??????

Throughout the house I heard *un*imagined voices shouting: "YES, WE *HEAR* YOU! GO . . . TO . . . BED!!"

But I couldn't. Not yet. So, very quietly, I played that ending over and over and over again. After I had recorded the song, people told me that the fade-out was longer than "Hey, Jude." My explanation was simple: People who are feeling heard don't ever want that feeling to go away.

And then the dairyman's daughter was gone. In my mind's eye I couldn't locate her anywhere. It surprised me when I heard myself sing what became the ending to the song:

After I've done my best,
I know you'll do the rest
Because I know you hear me.

The recording of the song sounded just like it had in my head, and I sent it to my wife and daughter who were on an educational tour together overseas. I mailed a copy so they'd have something to listen to on the long bus rides. Typical of my wife, she played the song for everyone and then called to tell me how much they had all responded to it.

She's never taken credit for the ending.

She should.

CHAPTER 12

SHE SEES A DIAMOND

The tip-off should have been the strategic placement of magazines all over the house. They were women's magazines—the kind guys don't usually pick up and read unless they're stuck at a beauty salon waiting for their wives and their cell phones are dead. *Women's Day, Ladies' Home Journal, Redbook,* each one of them had articles about how to tell if the honeymoon is over. Some of the magazines even had tests.

I should have realized that I was supposed to take one of these tests when the magazine was folded open to the test page and a freshly sharpened pencil was conveniently located nearby. But for weeks I missed the hint, even though there were copies on the nightstand, on the coffee table, in the kitchen, in the living room, family room, every room. I finally surrendered to one of the tests in the bathroom. Someone had hidden the *Reader's Digest.*

The questions hit on many aspects of marriage, but mostly the ones that had to do with keeping the fire of romance alive: Was there spontaneity, romance, passion, and soul-to-soul communication? According to my test score, the fire of marital bliss wasn't merely waning; the coals couldn't brown a marshmallow. I don't know if it was the competitor in me, or the sensitive husband I thought I always was, but the low score propelled me into action. I began researching the other women's magazines that were everywhere, seeking suggestions on how to put the fire back into a relationship. I was diligent in my research. For a family like ours, with three children under five, I learned that there would be special challenges to rekindling that fire. I took notes.

My game plan was really pretty simple, though it took me weeks to actually put it into practice. It included rewriting a song that I had written for Lynne when we were first falling in love. This was a tougher job than I thought because the only good thing about the original song was that it had her name in it eleven times. She always said she liked it—probably because there had never been a "Lynne" song on the radio—but trust me, it needed a lot of work.

Once the rewrite was completed, I moved on to gifts. Lynne had never been big on baubles, bangles, and bright shiny beads. She always seemed happiest when we found great deals at case-lot sales that included several months' worth of toilet paper. But a year's supply of canned goods and wet wipes didn't seem to be all that sexy, the more I thought about it, so I went to Nordstrom's. Everything I wanted to get her was more than I had to spend. I finally had them wrap up a gift certificate in a fancy silver box and asked when the half-yearly sale began.

Next, I tackled the element of surprise. The magazines were united on this: Surprise was crucial, and so were flowers.

So, I planned the moment: Operation Reclaim the Flame. It was a Wednesday afternoon about 3:30, and I came in the back door carrying fresh flowers and an ice-cold bottle of Pink Sparkling Catawba. Proceeded to lock the children in the bathroom and took my wife of seven years and pulled her to the piano. There I sang the song based on the melodic theme I'd written for her when we first dated as freshmen in college. I didn't just sing the song, I performed it, making sure that my thoughtful and sensitive side shone through. My goal was real tears by the second verse.

> She reaches part of me
> Underneath this ordinary man.
> She sees what I can be—
> Not what I've become but what I can.
> She sees a diamond deep in the rough of my soul;
> She says I'll see it too someday.
> She sees a diamond where all of the others just saw coal.
> She must see a million years away—
> But she keeps on loving me today.

I didn't hire a band to back me up, though there was the muffled sound of children in the bathroom chanting, "Daddy, let us out."

When I planned this all out in my mind, I didn't know whether Lynne would be so overwhelmed that she would start kissing me passionately right there on the piano bench, or if I would have to

74

stand up and kiss her because she'd be in such a state of shock. Neither happened.

"That's nice . . . are you finished?"

This wasn't how I'd envisioned this moment.

"Don't you see, Lynne, this is a new song based on the old one I wrote for you when we first met."

"I sort of liked the other one. It had my name in it."

The distant sound of flushing could be heard in the rhythmic S-O-S tradition.

"Lynne. Can't you see what I'm trying to do? The flowers, the bubbly stuff, the song . . ."

" . . . the locking of children in the bathroom . . ."

"I couldn't get a sitter. Look, I'm just doing what the magazines said. I'm trying to put some fire back into the marriage."

"Fire? You're singing me songs and bringing me flowers to put some fire back into our marriage? Listen, honey, if you really want to rock my world . . . *vacuum.*"

I'm sure my children wondered for years why the first thing their dad did when he got home from a business trip was to rev up the old Hoover. I suppose, now that they're grown, it won't damage them to know the truth.

Since that fateful day, I have reflected upon my experience and wondered if it wouldn't be helpful for a guy (like me, perhaps) to write an article to be read by other guys about keeping the fire in a relationship alive. The challenge would obviously be to speak in a language that would be not only understood but welcomed in the pages of such classic guy mags as *Popular Mechanics, Field and*

Stream, Sports Illustrated, and *Car & Driver.* If I were chosen for the task, my article might read something like this:

A Practical Guide to Understanding the Unknowable, or, How to Save a Marriage by Being Your Own Psychic

Chances are, if you've been married longer than an hour, your marriage is struggling and you don't even know it yet. You haven't been fully aware of all the problems you're having in your relationship (which your wife and her friends have been discussing over long lunches for months) because you've been too busy being a guy. You can be saved enormous grief and woe, not to mention experiencing an increase in the quality of desserts at your house, if you'll follow this practical guide to knowing the unknowable needs of your spouse:

1. Start Doing Stuff It Would Never Occur to You to Do
   - Pick up stuff that's lying around and put it in a less conspicuous place (like a laundry hamper or a garbage can).
   - Fold something, anything, that's in the dryer.
   - Take your plate and glass directly from the table to the dishwasher, leaving nothing to pile up in the sink.
   - Supervise putting your children in the tub and don't let them out until they're either clean or fully wrinkled.
   - Whatever you're getting from the kitchen that's edible, get more than you can possibly eat and cut it in bite-size pieces while saying, pleasantly, "I thought you'd like some of this."

2. If It Isn't Mechanical or Electronic, Don't Try to Fix It

If your wife has a problem with anything emotional or personal going on in her life, don't try to fix it. Avoid all attempts to figure out what to do. Just say things like: "You must feel terrible. How awful. I'm so sorry." Should she mention anything about the car or the dishwasher, feel free to get a wrench.

3. What You Think She Wants Is Probably What You Want

It's way more fun to give your wife something you want to give her than to find out what she really wants and needs. Therefore, if there's ever something you really, really think would make a perfect gift for your wife, ask yourself how often you'd borrow it if you could. If the answer is more than twice, choose something else.

4. Ask, Don't Tell

Smart married men through the ages hold these truths to be self-evident: It's a really good idea to ask. It's a really bad idea to tell. Whatever it is you want to tell your beloved that you're pretty sure is brilliant, don't say anything until you've asked at least twenty more minutes' worth of questions. If you're lucky, you'll have forgotten what you were going to say.

5. All Questions Are Really Requests

No matter what question the woman in your life asks you, it's really a request. "Are you hungry?" means "I want to eat." "Don't you like this?" means she wants you to tell her it's the most wonderful thing you've ever seen. Learn not to answer any of these questions but simply to respond to the request buried therein. This leads perfectly to the final point:

6. Speed's the Key

Whatever she says she wants, the speed with which you respond to her is more crucial than what you actually do. Be it a question that's a request, or a simple observation about how long it's been since she had a night away from the kids, the quicker you respond to whatever, the sooner you'll forget it wasn't what you wanted to do in the first place.

Now, lest you think that the guys who follow this practical guide are henpecked, wimpy little losers who don't know how to show a woman who's boss, let me direct your attention to the smiles on these men's faces. These are Cheshire-cat grins unseen in the rest of the male population. These guys are smiling like they're the only guys in the office who got a raise and can't tell anyone. These are the guys who don't talk about how happy their lives have become because those they'd tell would think they were lying. These are the guys who after a tough day at the office get the oft-neglected welcome-home neck rub. And these are the only guys on the planet who hear the words most men only dream of hearing, coming trippingly off the tongues of their adoring wives: "I threw a few frozen Snickers bars in your golf bag, babe . . . have a great round."

CHAPTER 13

SHE DOESN'T KNOW

I'm guessing you know a wonderful person or maybe several people who have no idea how wonderful they really are—in fact, it's almost impossible to tell them how great their terrificness is without them deflecting the compliment to someone they consider to be more worthy of the praise. And they're not being falsely modest or incredibly humble . . . they just don't believe it.

If you have someone like this in mind, I'll bet it's a woman. Might be your mom, might be a friend. Probably it's you.

I don't know why it is, but it's hard for most of us to see the positive impact of our everyday lives. We see the screwups pretty clearly, and we can remember them in detail for decades. It's the everyday, just regular good stuff about ourselves that never gets celebrated. Maybe that's why the movie *It's a Wonderful Life* keeps making us cry year after year.

I remember somebody telling me once that most songwriters

write only one or two songs and then basically write them over and over again, using different melodies and words. That might be true for me. Sometimes I feel like my internal wiring just picks up on others' goodness and flashes a message to the rest of my soul: *Righteousness alert! Warning, warning, you're standing on holy ground. Human compassion at three o'clock, completely unaware of its degrees of goodness!*

Along with this special wiring, I also have a radar for those who beat themselves up, and sometimes for the tiniest of mistakes. It isn't that these folks are by nature negative; they just have a magnifying glass in their brain when it comes to shortcomings.

Because I've seen this for so many years in so many different people—predominantly women I've known and admired and loved—I decided to smile at them and honor them in the same song.

A quarter to seven on a Thursday night:
She's running late again.
She got a ticket 'cause she ran the light
Racing to help a friend.
Then she remembers a promise made a couple of weeks before:
She'd bake the brownies for the PTA,
But she's run out of time, so she gets hers from the store.

A quarter to seven on a Friday night:
She's running late again,
Choosing a dress that will look just right
At the party she's throwing for him.
Living on rice cakes and Diet Coke,

She hasn't lost that much.
Her dress is too tight and her hair's a joke
But the party's a hit 'cause it had her magic touch.

But she doesn't know that she's an angel in disguise;
She doesn't know that we see heaven in her eyes.
She doesn't know that she's all right;
She might have been blinded by the light
Of all of the good that she does . . . but she doesn't know.

She's been worried about the kids next door
Since the breakup last fall.
Got them some T-shirts from a Hard Rock store
That they haven't worn at all.
Read in the paper about some plight
Plaguing a distant shore,
Gets out her checkbook and starts to write
And feels guilty she doesn't send more.

'Cause she doesn't know that she's an angel in disguise;
She doesn't know that we see heaven in her eyes.
She doesn't know that she's all right;
She might have been blinded by the light
Of all of the good that she does . . . but she doesn't know.

She doesn't notice all the good she does,
All she sees is where she failed her part.
Can't she see that we think she's a saint because
She's giving all she can straight from her heart?

81

A quarter to seven on a Sunday morn:
She's on her knees again.
Pleading for those who've been bruised and torn,
She's asking for help for them.
She has a rather extensive list of those she's been praying for,
But when she remembers the ones she's missed,
She feels so sorry once more.

'Cause she doesn't know that she's an angel in disguise;
She doesn't know that we see heaven in her eyes.
She doesn't know that she's all right;
She might have been blinded by the light
Of all of the good that she does,
But she doesn't see it because
She hits a traffic jam on a carpool morn
And feels guilty what she's thinkin' as she honks her horn.
She wrote a sympathy note to her dear friend Grace
But got it lost somewhere in cyberspace.
And at the charity auction when she wanted to help,
She raised her hand so many times
She sort of bid against herself.
She got the casserole made
For her friend who was sick,
But then apologized
Because the crust was too thick.
She's running to the soccer and the baseball games,
She cheers for the teams but forgets their names.

She doesn't know that she's a miracle
She doesn't know her love is lyrical
She doesn't know this song's for her to hear
She doesn't know that we are so sincere
She doesn't know that she's the best
She doesn't know she's passed the test
She doesn't know
She doesn't know
She doesn't know!

Could this possibly be you that this song is about? Could *you* be the angel in disguise in someone else's life? Are you so busy doin' the best you can that you're blinded by the light of your own goodness?

If you're answering *no* to these questions and making a mental note of all the things on your list that haven't yet been accomplished, will you just stop it, at least for a moment, and work with me on this.

Pretend for now, just pretend, that you're the person in this song.

Quit laughing, we're pretending. Get out the music and put it on your stereo. Crank it up and listen—not with your ears, but with your heart.

I'll wait.

There was a moment, wasn't there, while you were pretending, when something happened that was so touching it almost hurt to keep listening.

The thought, "Could it be true?" crossed your mind. Could you actually be that wonderful and that stupid at the same time?

Yes, you could, and you are, and that's one of the reasons people love you so much. You're a human being who makes mistakes and falls short and can't quite get as much done as you want to in a day and guess what? If you weren't here we'd be crying our eyes out because we'd miss you so much. We'd miss the way you laugh and the way you get mad at people who hurt others. We'd miss the stories you tell of your misadventures. We'd miss how blessed we feel when you pray for us. We'd miss the look on your face when you scoop the hot fudge directly out of the little pitcher and take it straight. We'd miss the way you sing along with Celine in the car when you don't think anyone's watching. We'd miss the way your eyes look when you've heard about someone's heartache and the way your jaw tightens when you want to get revenge. We'd miss the brownies that you burned and the Mint Milanos you bought to replace them. We couldn't stand watching *Sleepless in Seattle* without you. We'd miss the things we learned because of you. We'd miss the way we've been loved by you, even when you didn't think you told us often enough. And we'd have felt totally cheated if we'd never known you. In fact, the world wouldn't have a chance at being truly wonderful for us if you weren't in it, being you.

Now that you've pretended that all of this is true, take a deep breath and come back to reality.

Guess what? The truth hasn't changed.

Let yourself believe it.

CHAPTER 14

IT'S NOT LOVE

September 1970, a week before I started college, the phone rang. "Hey, Mike, it's Larry. Friday night these two girls from Thailand are going to be in town. One is the great-niece of an old crippled woman my dad used to work with at the university, and I think they've talked about getting us together for years . . ."

"You and the crippled gal?"

"No, no, me and the niece from Thailand. Anyway, there's a dinner at the old lady's house because her arthritis is so bad she really can't get around. In fact, her ninety-year-old mother takes care of her, and she'll be there too, and I understand that if she likes you she takes her teeth out."

"The girl from Thailand?"

"No, the old woman."

"The one with the arthritis?"

"No, her mother. Wanna come?"

"Larry, I've been dreaming of a night like this all my life."

Larry picked me up about six-fifteen. On our way to the blind date of my dreams, we created a little code, like signals in baseball. If things went the way I imagined they might, I would do a yawn and a stretch and remind Larry about our "early hike" in the morning (wink, wink), and we'd thank our ancient and infirm hostesses, bow with our hands together, and be at the movies by nine.

We were greeted at the door by a large old woman with false teeth. I probably shouldn't have noticed that those teeth didn't seem to fit very comfortably, but I did. I got the feeling that the only time she put them in was for church on Sundays or when company called.

"Come on in, boys. I'm Nanny." When she waved us in, her grandma arms flapped proudly, uncovered by her short-sleeved dress. "I'll get the girls." She left us alone in the entryway long enough for us to practice our signal a couple of times and notice the pictures. There were lots of pictures in that hall—photos framed and hanging on the walls or perched on antique bookshelves. Several were of military men in uniform; a few were of Nanny in Europe with people I did not know; and there was one high school graduation picture of a green-eyed beauty I couldn't take my eyes off.

Then, as if by some miracle, the picture in the entryway came to life before my very eyes: an American girl in a brown Thai silk outfit, with a hairdo that had to have been inspired by Ann-Margret in *Bye Bye Birdie*.

I couldn't breathe. I lost all control of autonomic nervous

system functions. This would have been fine had I simply been paralyzed by her adorableness, but instead I became afflicted with a not-so-rare disorder often contracted by young men in the presence of babes: a malady known as IOMS, or Impress-O-Matic Syndrome.

It's a sad thing to see, really. A fairly pleasant and normal young man suddenly has an uncontrollable desire to play every piece he's ever learned on the piano while telling every joke he's ever heard. Twice. Advanced cases of IOMS have been known to trigger IOMSeizures, causing uncontrollable bragging about Pinewood Derby cars, the number of merit badges earned as a Boy Scout, and the talent award received in junior high for a performance of Bill Cosby's routine about Noah and the ark. Personal space is invaded, friends are shoved aside, and, in extreme instances, IOMS causes shameless kissing up to old and arthritic ladies. It isn't pretty.

Everyone who has ever suffered from a severe case of the syndrome hopes against hope that the one who has ignited the bizarre behavior will know that only her response can administer the cure.

The interesting thing about IOMS is that, like drugs, it can burn itself out, and through sheer exhaustion one has to shut down for a while. It was during one of these periods that I got to discover that I was in the presence of greatness.

The crippled aunt, Louise Browning, was one of the most beloved teachers of social work in the history of the University of Utah. She was wise and witty and wonderful—wonderful enough to see past the temporary insanity of my IOMS and find something about me worth loving. And her mother, Nanny, was a remarkable woman as well, not simply because of the way she cared for her daughter, but because of the way she had of caring for strangers and making them feel comfortable. After I'd played *Für Elise* one too many times, she put her arm around me and her teeth in a jar.

As you can certainly imagine, there were no signals given or references made to any "early hikes" the next morning. After dinner, Larry and I took the American girls from Thailand on a tour of the town. Intermittently my IOMS would flare up, however, and I would find myself doing the strangest things. At Fendall's ice cream parlor I slipped a five-dollar bill to the waitress and told her that I was going to "steal" one of the long-handled spoons we used to eat our burnt almond fudge malt. Just to prove to you how unbalanced IOMS can make a person, I remembered hearing about a guy who stole a spoon from an ice cream parlor, had it engraved, and turned it into a bracelet for his girlfriend, *and I actually thought this was a cool idea!* I'm telling you, IOMS is sick and it's sad.

I suppose I grabbed at the spoon idea because, as the evening wore on, I became more and more desperate. I knew I was out of my league with this girl. She was beyond perfect, and once she hit the campus of the college we would both be attending, she'd be swept away in a New York minute. So I scrambled to find some way to make her need to see me again. When we drove the girls up to the state capitol so they could see a panoramic view of the city, I finalized my plan.

There were several sunflowers growing wild on the side of the hill, and in a dramatic flare I grabbed one and wrapped it around the spoon I had paid for but pretended I'd stolen from the ice cream store. (This is how a goody-two-shoes guy misguidedly tries to go for the James Dean appeal.)

"This sort of sums up our evening together," I said, handing her my gift.

"A sunflower wrapped around an ice cream spoon? What does it mean?"

"Next time I see you, I'll tell you."

Of course, I had *no* idea what it meant. I figured something would come to me. Point was, I *had* to see her again before she married some hunk in med school, and this was all I could come up with.

A few days later I found myself wandering around campus hoping to run into the only great blind date I would ever know. I thought I saw her on the way to the library and was about to approach her, but then I recoiled and panicked. What if she asked me about the sunflower and spoon? What was I going to say? I'd have to come up with something, anything, so I wouldn't be caught in my desperate little web of romantic deception.

Come on, brain, think of something fast. She's turning this way. Quick, run.

But upon seeing her there, I was a deer caught in the headlights. I couldn't move as she approached. She was wearing a coy, self-satisfied smile.

"I figured it out . . . the spoon and sunflower thing you gave me. I know what it means."

"Really?"

"Yes. I talked to my great-aunt, and we saw the creative

symbolism in your gift. You see, a spoon is a form of measurement, and a sunflower always follows the light and warmth of the sun. And the way we can measure the growth of a friendship is by the light and warmth that grows within us with each new memory we make."

I stared at her for at least thirty seconds. "How did you know?"

I was in love. And the more I was around her and learned how she felt about things and saw how she treated people, the more I loved her. I tried to impress her by writing her songs and poetry and taking her to concerts. She responded by listening to the songs, reading the poems, and telling me that someday I'd be up on that concert stage and people would be clapping for me. But the most wonderful thing she did for me was find a way to let me know that I didn't have to try so hard. Turns out she was plenty impressed and would like it if we could just be ourselves together. This proved to be the truest and finest cure of IOMS known to man.

I married her. Lynne Louise, the reason my heart had a song.

> *She is the sunset that every photographer dreams of finding.*
> *She is the moon that brings lovers together at night.*
> *She's a cool breeze on hot summer days,*
> *She's the brush strokes in every Monet, and*
> *She's the girl no one really believes they'll ever find.*
> *But she lives, somewhere in every man's heart*
> *And every man's mind.*
> *She knows just what to do;*
> *She's too good to be true.*

I can't understand
How this girl could be right here next to me,
Holding my hand . . .

I continued to be crazy about her in a way many of my associates told me was unsustainable throughout a long marriage. But they said that, I believed, because they obviously were married to lesser women. If they were married to my Lynne, their hearts would still race when they got a call from their wife.

My heart stopped racing in 1986. I woke up one morning and it was gone and I couldn't will it back. I didn't care anymore about the person who had meant more to me than anyone or anything on earth. I panicked.

I thought maybe it was the years of PMS that finally got to me. All men who've been married to women who have suffered from industrial-strength premenstrual syndrome never need wonder what it's like to live in polygamy because they already have. Every two weeks a different woman shows up.

Maybe it was stress. Maybe it was an approaching midlife crisis. Whatever it was, it was real and it scared me. I got the name of a counselor who had helped a friend of mine, and I called for an appointment.

I canceled and rescheduled a bunch of times. Shouldn't I be able to take care of this myself? I mean, I can't drill my own teeth or prescribe antibiotics for pneumonia or replace a clogged artery, but this emotional marital disorder should have been something I could just work out alone.

91

But it got worse, and I couldn't fix the problem alone, so finally Lynne and I arrived at the therapist's office.

"Look, Dr.—"

"Call me Ken."

"Okay, Ken, I just want you to know that we're here because there's nothing more important to us than this relationship, and it doesn't matter how much this costs or how long it takes. We promised that we'd love each other forever, and something has gone wrong, and so we've come for some professional help. Take your time. I understand that things like this don't change overnight. She's struggled with PMS for years. Do what you need to do. I'll be supporting you both, every step of the way. Go ahead: Fix her."

The therapist just looked at me. He wanted to make sure he'd heard me correctly. "Fix . . . her?"

I had the feeling he was trying to give me a way out, but I was too big a mess to take it. I just nodded.

"Well, we might get to her in a few . . . *months!*"

Now I was the one trying to make sure I'd heard correctly. Was he referring to me? *Me?* I was the guy who won awards making commercials about how to stay in love with your wife. I was the guy who sensitively wrote songs and brought his PMS-ing woman flowers. I *vacuumed!*

"What do you mean, a few months?"

"Look, Michael, seems to me, you're the one with the problem. You're the one who can't feel anything for the woman he's been crazy about since he was eighteen years old. Maybe it would help if we could find out why you shut down that part of yourself."

92

I started to twitch. It's never a good thing to twitch in front of a psychologist who reads body language the way most of us read *Newsweek*.

"What's the matter, Michael? You seem uncomfortable."

"You think it'll take months?"

"Who knows? I don't really believe in spending years and years of people's lives and taking all their money just to help them find out they were poorly potty trained. But this may not be something we can fix today."

"But it *can* be fixed, right?" I needed some reassurance.

"Do you know anything about cars, Michael? In your spare time, when you're not writing songs or writing films or directing commercials, do you rebuild engines?"

"I can barely tell the difference between the dipstick for the oil and the transmission fluid."

"So, when you drop off your car to get fixed, you don't hang around and tell the mechanic what to do while he's under the hood."

"No."

"He'd probably double the price if you did. Well, the same is true here. I'll tinker a bit under the hood, see what I can find, and let you know. Okay?"

I wondered if shrinks had diagnostic probes I should know about. Turns out they do, only you can't see them.

The doctor went to work on me. Lynne was with me during most of the sessions. It was a remarkable process. As it happened, the things I was most afraid of facing were not as scary as I imagined when I saw them in the light of truth.

My therapist taught me a great deal through telling me stories and inviting me to read books that could open my heart and mind to the truth. The guy changed my life and taught me principles that didn't just save my marriage but deeply and profoundly enriched it.

As our therapy sessions began, I remember calling the children together and telling them that, as much as I loved them, they came fifth. They were terrific people, but they weren't the most important thing in my life—their mother was, and she and I were going to learn how to love each other better. I didn't care if the Cub Scouts got a new Webelos leader or the Sunday School picked a better teacher, didn't care if they fired me at work or banned me from the studio, didn't care if the neighborhood branded me as antisocial. The first four things on my priority list would be: my wife, their mother, their mother and me, and me and their mother. Children came fifth.

They seemed to get it. We didn't lose them by focusing so keenly on our marriage . . . in fact, they flourished as we did. The happier Mom and Dad were with each other, the better they did. Emotional scarring did *not* take place when we missed a school play or a recital or a ball game. The kids just told everyone who asked them where their folks were that they were in therapy, and it was okay because they came fifth anyway.

Marriage counseling changed us both, along with our definition of *love*. We recently commemorated twenty-eight years of marriage and thirty-two since that blind date. When the professional therapy ended, it seemed fitting and natural to celebrate our journey together with a couple of songs. Deep in my heart I hoped the songs I had written for my wife would impress her. Turns out, they didn't need to.

He's counting the hours until he sees her face again.
Three hours is a million years; he just can't wait till then.
Last night was electric, she knocked him off his feet—
He's been down this road before; he knows this side of the street.
With all of his heart he believes that it's love,
But somehow he ought to see:
It's not love till it's been through a storm.
It's not love till it's died and reborn.
It's not love till it comes to an end
And still you have faith to try once again;
Till then . . . it's not love.
It's not love just because it feels right.
It's not love until you've sacrificed.
It's not love until we've healed the hurt.
It's not love till we both make it work.
It's not love till we've seen all the flaws.
It's not love till we've given our all.

CHAPTER 15

IF ONLY YOU BELIEVE
IN YOURSELF

I figured she was either an airhead or just disinterested in things academic. It didn't occur to me that my six-year-old daughter might be having petit mal seizures—as many as forty or fifty a day. When the doctor showed us the chart of my girl's abnormal brain waves, he gave us the good news along with the bad.

"The good news is that there are medications that can help your daughter avoid the spacing out episodes known as petit mal seizures. The bad news is that we won't know which drug will have the least objectionable side effects until after we've tried it for a while. We'll do our best and hope we get lucky."

We weren't lucky. The side effect of the first medicine was terrible nightmares. As a result, Meggan tried to avoid the bad dreams by not going to sleep at night, which in turn caused her to fall asleep in class. The boys in her class teased her mercilessly.

The next medication created an Incredible Hulk girl with such aggressive behavior that the guys picked her first for their side in football. The girls in her class teased her mercilessly.

Other medications, other side effects, same results: fewer seizures, more ridicule. It was painful for the parents. I can only imagine how hard it was for a little girl.

As it turned out, we left the big city and moved to the country about the time our daughter caught the right wave of medication. She approached the move to a new place with apprehension.

"Daddy, I think moving is like repentance."

"How so, Meggan?"

"Nobody knows anything bad about me. It's like I get a clean slate. I just hope I don't mess up this time, because if you make a mistake, they don't ever let you forget."

She said it earnestly and with a melancholy a nearly nine-year-old shouldn't have had to experience.

We were living in a little rental behind the bowling alley, waiting for the permits to build our own home on an alfalfa patch on the outskirts of town. Our daughter played tentatively in the neighborhood and, I suspect, looked a bit like a frightened refugee from another country.

Three days after we moved in, a man and a woman knocked on our door. The woman spoke first.

"We'd like to welcome you to the neighborhood. We don't do cookies, we do cattle . . . here's a roast."

The woman handed me a lump of meat wrapped in white butcher paper. I was speechless. My mother never trained me in "roast reception." What was I supposed to say? "Nice rump"?

"Thanks, this is really_____" I could have filled in the blank with any number of words—*thoughtful, considerate, neighborly, nice*—but I went another way.

"This is really . . . heavy." I meant it like it was a good thing, and, bless their hearts, they took it as a compliment.

"Mr. McLean?" There was a long pause. I didn't know if the man was trying to remember something he'd practiced before he came, or if I had just not yet adjusted to the pace of a small, rural town. "My name's Ollie, and this here's Susan, and besides bringin' the beef we was hopin' you could do us a big favor."

"What would that be, Ollie?" I braced myself for the request, picturing images of mule teams and barn raisings, for some reason—but it wasn't that.

"Well, my horse Poco ain't missed ridin' in the kids' rodeo in twenty-three years. But this year our daughter Brooke busted up her leg and won't be able to ride him . . ."

Ollie took a moment to pause. It seemed to me like it was a brief mourning I didn't understand. Then he took a breath and carried on.

"And it would be a shame for Poco to not be in the fair this year, so I was wondering . . . I know this is a lot to ask of someone who just moved in, but I was wondering if you could do me a big favor and let me give your daughter my horse for the summer."

If I was inexperienced in roast reception, it was nothing compared to this.

"Ollie . . . I'd be . . . and I'm sure my girl would be . . . more than . . . happy to . . . a . . . well . . . help you out . . . but we . . . I mean . . . I don't really know . . . much about . . . horses. I'm from New Jersey."

98

Ollie nodded. "That's pretty obvious, sir, if you don't mind my sayin' so. But you don't have to worry about a thing. I've got saddle and tack that'll fit your girl just perfect. I'll get her to Red Ribbon Riders every Wednesday and she'll be just fine. Poco's a good ol' boy and he runs them barrels good. Thanks for helpin' me out."

Helping him out? Right. I'm doing Ollie a big favor by letting him give my nine-year-old daughter his horse for the summer and training her how to ride him. Well, God bless the Ollie Clydes of this world who don't just show up and give us cookies and tell us that if we need anything we should feel free to call, because *we never call*. I mean, honestly, what was I going to do, pick up the phone and say, "Hey, we just moved in. We've got a kid with no self-esteem . . . got a horse?" Of course not. We don't ask because we don't want to owe anybody; we don't want to be beholden to anyone; we want to carry our own weight and take care of ourselves; it's the way we were raised. But you gotta love the guy who sees a scared kid moping around the neighborhood and just knows what she needs and finds a way to give it to her. It's been nearly twenty years since this happened, and I still get emotional thinking about it.

What chokes me up is remembering how learning to ride that horse made my daughter a new person. There's something about a nine-year-old and a horse that's . . . well, it's almost spiritual.

When Meggan rode down Main Street in the parade and gave the cowgirl wave, it was a magic moment. I think I know how Steve Young's parents must have felt the first time they saw their boy walk onto a football field.

The confidence she showed on that horse started to spill over into the rest of her life. She didn't seem as afraid of everything as she had been before. She seemed to know how to rein in and direct the emerging young woman within, in much the same way as she guided Poco down Main Street.

I thought she had mastered her fears until the night before the kids' rodeo, when she opened up to her city-slicker dad. "I'm scared, Daddy. What if I fall?"

I was so naive about rodeos, I offered this helpful thought. "You know, Meggan, I think for the kids' rodeo they fluff up the dirt somehow."

She was not reassured.

You know, when Jesus taught us to be like little children, he didn't mean second and third graders. I wanted to go strangle every kid who had ever teased or hurt or ridiculed my daughter and make them apologize for what they'd done. And after that passed, I wanted to apologize myself to every person I'd ever teased or hurt or ridiculed. And then, after *that*, I wanted to give my girl something that would help her get through this thing.

I wanted to say: "Meggan, so much of life is a plot to rob us of our self-esteem. Just when you start thinking you're somebody and can do things in this old world, something comes along to tell you that you can't. I don't care whether you're a nine-year-old girl waiting to ride the barrels in the kids' rodeo, or a seventeen-year-old who doesn't get a part in the play, or a thirty-seven-year-old whose husband leaves her with three kids and she has to figure out how to support them. It's all a plot to convince us that we're no good and that we're only kidding ourselves to think that we could be something and make a difference with our lives."

But it's easier to write it down and make it sound good (and rhyme) sometimes than it is to say. So I wrote Meggan a song to try to explain how I felt. She liked the song I wrote for her, but she seemed to understand that the song didn't have anything to do with her increased self-esteem. That came from the red ribbon she won that afternoon, and the way she felt every time she guided Ollie's horse where she wanted it to go.

What I learned from watching her is that nobody can give you a feeling of self-worth. Nobody can preach it to you or teach it to you or sing it to you. It's a victory and a gift you give yourself.

I think of this song not as one that inspires self-esteem, but as a reminder of the risks we all must be willing to take to achieve it:

Anxiously a cowgirl sits, waiting for her number to be called,
Clinging to the horn of her worn saddle,
Saying prayers that she won't fall.
Staring at the barrels in the small-town rodeo,
She's awfully scared but hopes it doesn't show.
In the stands she sees the fans who came to see
Her race in record time.
It's tough to keep your cool with all this pressure,
Especially when you're nine.
Then someone calls her number and it's time for her to ride;
She strains to hear the words again her father said last night:

"If only you believe in yourself,
I know you can achieve.
If only you believe in yourself,
You won't be scared."

Anxiously a singer sits, waiting for a chance to sing her song,
Hoping if she hears them say, "You're not that good,"
She'll know deep down they're wrong.
One more bad audition and she's vowed she'll pack it in,
But just before she sings, she tries to hear those words again:
"If only you believe in yourself,
I know you can achieve.
If only you believe in yourself,
You won't be scared."

Anxiously a woman sits, waiting for her number to be called,
Clinging to the telephone receiver on a table in the hall.
Staring at the mirror above her radio,
She's awful scared and fears that it may show.
Losing all your confidence is what comes after losing all your pride,
And losing what you thought was love
Makes loving once again so hard to try.
Then someone calls her number and she fears she'll fail again,
Until she hears the words she's known
Since she was nine or ten . . .
"If only you believe in yourself,
I know you can achieve.
If only you believe in yourself,
You won't be scared."

CHAPTER 16

FROM GOD'S ARMS

I got a call from a young woman who wanted to write a song with me. She said that she'd been touched by a particular song I had written and felt like I could help her with a special composition. I think I said something about not being a great doubles player.

"That's okay. You can write the song yourself. I just need some help. You see, I'm pregnant and I'm not married, and after great soul-searching I've decided to place my baby for adoption. I was hoping you could write a song that I could sing to the family I'm giving my baby to."

My first instinct was to run away from this. How could *I* possibly know what it felt like to be an unwed pregnant woman about to give her child to someone else? How could *I* ever truly understand her position? *I* couldn't write the song she wanted. *I* would look foolish if *I* tried. Let's see, just how many other *I* concerns should I recall here? When this wasn't about me anymore (and I stopped racking my brain for the names of women songwriters she should call), I could concentrate on really listening to this birth-mother-to-be.

She talked about what had led to her decision and told me it was because she felt that she couldn't give her baby what he deserved: a home, a family, a father. It wasn't the material things she was worried about, it was the spiritual ones she felt so unable to give her unborn child.

"There's this really amazing couple. They're spiritual, they're loving, they're totally committed to each other, and they've been waiting for a baby for nine years. I'm sure they are the right ones to get this baby home."

I thought she meant to say that she had found a couple who could *give* her baby a home, but when I asked her about it, she explained: "They'll give him a home so they can get him Home . . . you know, to God."

The expectant mother believed that her baby's spirit was coming directly from heaven, and that as the one who was bringing that life into this world, it was her responsibility to do all she could to help her child learn how to return to his heavenly home. Her assessment of her own situation led her to realize that, as agonizing as the decision was, when she put the child's best interest ahead of her own, she knew what she had to do.

We were having this conversation over the phone, so I couldn't see who I was speaking to. The picture of her I had in my mind at the beginning of the conversation was much different from the one that was developing the longer we spoke. As I listened to this young woman's plea for help, my paradigm of unwed mothers was radically altered. She told me she was afraid this baby might grow up think-ing that if his own birth mother would give him away, he probably wasn't worth very much.

"I've got to find a way to let this child know that I'm doing this because it's the only way I know how to show him how much he was loved by me from the start. The other thing I want the baby to know is that he isn't genetically immoral. I made a terrible mistake, but, Michael, he's got to know that the one who brought him into the world wasn't a sleaze."

As she spoke, I felt ashamed of myself for all the times I had felt smugly superior to "those kinds of girls" who get in trouble. I felt sick to my stomach because so often in my life I'd been so willing to cast the first stone. But all of that was melting away.

She mentioned that she'd kept a journal through the experience and that many of her thoughts and feelings in it might help me with the song. I told her that songs were gifts, and that I didn't always know when they would arrive, but that I would work on it and try to get myself ready to hear it when it came.

A few months later, the song arrived. The impact of that initial conversation and the discussions that followed must have filled my creative subconscious until it overflowed one night in my studio at home. I called my friend to tell her that the song's water had bro-ken. While it was so fresh and new, I wanted to sing it to her over the phone and see if it was even close to capturing the feelings of her heart. With the phone in the crook of my neck, a yellow legal pad filled with scribbled-over and scratched-out lyrics propped on the piano, and my fingers in the key of C, I sang:

With so many wrong decisions in my past, I'm not quite sure
If I can ever hope to trust my judgment anymore.
But lately I've been thinking, 'cause it's all I've had to do,
And in my heart I feel that I should give this child to you.
And maybe you can tell your baby
When you love him so, that he's been loved before
By someone who delivered your son
From God's arms to my arms to yours.

If you choose to tell him, or if he wants to know
How the one who gave him life could bear to let him go,
Just tell him there were sleepless nights
I prayed and paced the floors
And knew the only peace I'd find is if this child was yours.
And maybe you can tell your baby
When you love him so, that he was loved before
By someone who delivered your son
From God's arms to my arms to yours.

Now I know you don't have to do this,
But could you kiss him once for me
The first time that he ties his shoes or falls and skins his knee?
And could you hold him twice as long
When he makes his mistakes
And tell him that he's not alone—
Sometimes that's all it takes.
I know how much he'll ache.

Well, this may not be the answer
For another girl like me,
And I'm not on a soapbox saying how we all should be.
I'm just trusting in my feelings
And I'm trusting God above,
And I'm trusting you can give this baby
Both his mothers' love.
And maybe you can tell your baby
When you love him so, that he was loved before
By someone who delivered your precious one
From God's arms
To my arms
To yours.

When I finished singing, there was silence on the other end of the phone. After a long pause, my friend spoke. "How did you know? That's exactly right, but how did you know?"

The truth was, I didn't know. I couldn't have known. My own experience and even fairly well-trained powers of observation didn't know. But I wasn't writing this song for myself. I wasn't hoping it would make it on the charts someday. I'd been transformed by the power of someone's example, and I yearned to follow that example of being more concerned about someone else than about myself. Because I was using what gifts I'd been given to help someone carry out the unselfish desires of her heart, something beyond my set of skills was clearly at work.

We arranged for her to come into the studio and sing the song for the family she was giving her baby to. It was five days, I think, after the baby was born, and she placed the pictures of the child on a music stand next to the words she was singing. It was a good thing I knew the chords by heart because I wouldn't have been able to see them written down on paper for the tears.

I had never planned to release a recording of "From God's Arms to My Arms to Yours." It seemed too personal, too private. Things changed, however, a few months later when I felt impressed to share the song during a concert in a small rural town. When the program was over, I discovered that the song had affected more people in the audience than I had ever anticipated—from the adopted teenagers to their parents to the pregnant girls who were trying to decide what to do with the babies they were carrying but hadn't told anyone about.

To protect the privacy of the people involved, the song was recorded by a gifted studio singer who knew nothing of those whose story had brought it to life. It was the last song I put on the *One Heart in the Right Place* album.

After its release, I found a whole new world of friends, and the song bound us together in tender ways. I heard from birth mothers, adoptive mothers, grandparents, teenagers, adoption agencies, celebrities, and friends. The song moved in mysterious ways. Several years after it had been recorded, I was in Toronto, Canada, directing some commercials for a water heater company. They called me because they wanted people to get emotional about their water heaters. One of the production assistants who drove me back and forth to the set mentioned one day that she was adopted.

I told her that I had written a song about adoption called "From God's Arms to My Arms to Yours."

She pulled the car over. "You wrote 'From God's Arms to My Arms to Yours'?" I wondered how she knew about this song. It hadn't been released in Canada. It wasn't a commercial hit that got airplay. How could she have known about this song, so far away from its birthplace?

"Last year, my birth mother found me. She sought me out, came to Toronto, and gave me a tape with your song on it. I didn't know who had written it or who was singing because it was a copy of a copy of a copy."

Songwriters *love* hearing that.

The twenty-six-year-old continued: "My birth mother told me that for twenty-six years she had feared that I didn't know why she did what she did, and that this song was her heart. I listen to it almost every day. How can I thank you?"

"No need to thank me. The one to thank is the one who loved you enough to give you a home she couldn't provide."

The song acknowledges that adoption may not be the answer for everyone, but those I've met who felt adoption was their answer always add: It was an answer to prayer.

CHAPTER 17

A NEW KIND OF
LOVE SONG

One of the great perks of being a songwriter is having so many friends who can sing. Not being a big fan of my own voice, I've recorded almost all my songs with other artists doing the vocals: pop singers, folksingers, theatrical singers, operatic singers, rock singers, jingle singers, choir singers, rhythm and blues singers, country singers, and gospel singers. Several years ago one of my favorite gospel singers invited our family to a revival at her church.

The place had room for about three hundred and fifty people, but I'm certain there were closer to five hundred at the service. There were only eleven white faces in the congregation, seven of which belonged to my family. The singers bore their testimonies of Jesus in song, and they rocked the building. The band was tight, the choirs were together, the harmonies were classic, and the soloists were passionate and inspired.

It was unlike anything my kids were used to, and I watched them closely to see how they responded as each group took center stage.

The service was moving, in more ways than one. There was something going on in that room besides the rhythm of a gospel backbeat. We were experiencing singing that was coming from a place in the soul many of us have never admitted existed, much less visited regularly. Tears of gratitude, adoration, and love came pouring out along with the heavenly acrobatic vocalizations of those feelings.

Walking out of the service, my seven-year-old said, "Dad, how come we don't sing like that?"

I thought about it for a minute and replied: "Because we're white."

He was a little embarrassed by my answer. He was seriously wanting to know why our family, when we were at our church, didn't sing with the same amount of passion and intensity and uninhibited celebration as the people in that meeting.

I tried to defend the culture I was bringing him up in, explaining that spirituality has many faces and that sometimes our sweetest feelings about the Lord come to us in quiet, reverent moments.

"But we don't *ever* have the other moments like they do. Don't we have as much to be happy about?"

Then he gave a little list of all the things he'd been taught that were the core assets of our family's chosen faith and asked, "Shouldn't we be singin' like we mean it?"

He was right. We should be singing like we mean it. But what does that mean? For songs of praise, must one style fit all? Try as I may, I doubt if I'll ever be able to sing like my gospel singing friends who invited us to their church. And try as they might, the music where I worship each week may never feel familiar to their souls.

I remember that during the service we attended, someone said, "If we ain't livin' what we're singin', it's nothing but noise." That and my discussion with my son got me seriously wondering what God thinks about how His children sing about Him and to Him. If a song of the heart is truly a prayer unto God, which songs are reaching farther into heaven? Are the greatest songs of praise to the Lord not even songs at all, but little acts of compassion, moments of kindness, evidence of genuine love?

Sometimes I think God may have given us the ability to make music not because He needs to hear it but because we need to feel it. Maybe the singing of worship songs is solely meant to give greater spiritual focus to, and increase the commitment of, the singer.

The real question for me is, what kind of song can I sing? I love this song a lot because it keeps reminding me that in the end, true love isn't something we say, it isn't something we sing, it's something we do.

> *I want to sing a new kind of love song.*
> *I want to sing with a voice that's new.*
> *I want to sing with so much feeling*
> *My love for you shines through.*
> *But writers with gifts I've not been given*

Have given their all to find the perfect phrase,
And voices that sound like angels from heaven
Have already sung your praise.
But if you could turn the water into wine,
And find some hope for a misguided life like mine,
If you could know my weaknesses,
Yet help me to be strong,
Then you could hear a symphony in just a simple song.
I love you. I love you.
And even though I know a song will never really do,
I'll make my life my song of love,
Every day of my life will be my song of love,
My life must be
My song of love for you . . .
'Cause I want to sing a new king of love song.

CHAPTER 18

SAFE HARBORS

At the time of this writing, the world is at war. Those who aren't in actual combat on some foreign soil are fighting about whether the war is justified. Around the world there is much contention and heated debate about the just use of power. The wars and rumors of more wars are enough to make any rational person sick at heart and sad for the state of the world.

I've watched, along with people all over the world, the newscasts from so many different countries and ached for those lost souls searching for a home, a place to rebuild their lives.

I remember during one of the televised refugee crises I told my wife I felt the need to do something. Should we send money? Clothing? Food? What?

Come to find out, my wife had already participated with compassionate women across the globe in united humanitarian efforts to ease the suffering. But I didn't feel like I could knit bandages or sew quilts. What could I do?

"You really want to help the refugees?" she asked sincerely, without a hint of judgment.

"Yes, I really do."

She then took me by the hand, led me to the window, and pointed to a house down the street. "If you want to help some refugees," she said, " start with them."

What my wife was teaching me was that wars aren't just being fought "out there." It isn't just families who have tragically lost loved ones to falling skyscrapers or guided missiles that are in mourning. In every neighborhood in every community in the world, somebody's carrying some grief, some fear, some sadness, some unspeakable injustice, some unbearable horror—and all are in need of a safe harbor of the heart.

There, in a little brick house not even a thousand yards from mine, was a torn and broken family, a tragic teen suicide, siblings at risk, and enough heartache to fill a continent.

> *There are refugees among us*
> *That are not from foreign shores,*
> *And the battles they are waging*
> *Are from very private wars.*
> *And there are no correspondents*
> *Documenting all their grief,*
> *But these refugees among us*
> *All are yearning for relief.*

Five houses up the street there's a different story being told. The darkness and anxiety have been growing for years. Had our neighbor had a physical illness as severe as her mental one, she would have died years ago, but hour by hour she keeps looking for a reason to hang on one more day.

Next door, a mother worries not because her child battles too many feelings but too few. How does she reach beyond the vacant, distant looks and make a meaningful emotional connection with the one she brought into the world?

There are refugees among us.
They don't carry flags or signs.
They are standing right beside us
In the market checkout lines.
And the wars that they've been fighting
Will not be televised,
But the story of their need for love
Is written in their eyes.

And then there are those who carry burdens so secret, so private, so unthinkable that their only way of coping is to pretend that what happened never did.

Can you see through their disguises?
Can you hear what words won't tell?
Some are losing faith in heaven
'Cause their life's a living hell.
Is there anyone to help those

116

Who have nowhere else to flee?
For the only arms protecting them
Belong to you and me.
This is a call to arms, to reach out and to hold
The evacuees from the dark.
This is a call to arms, to lead anguished souls
To safe harbors of the heart.
Can you feel the pleas of the refugees
For safe harbors of the heart?

I have seen all around me people who have built those safe harbors—not with bricks and mortar but with compassion and concern. I've seen people extending themselves without butting in. Comforting without preaching. Healing with hugs and empowering with pot roast. And for as much unseen pain and suffering as there is going on all around us, there is an equal if not greater amount of love and service that never finds a spot on the nightly news . . . but if you listen you can hear it. I know I can, and it inspires me. It's the most glorious song I've ever heard, and it's flowing like a river from the human spirit into safe harbors of the heart everywhere.

CHAPTER 19

I'M JUST ONE OF THE NINETY AND NINE

I'm not a morning person. The only 5:30 I'm very familiar with is the one in the afternoon. I join other non-morning people in proclaiming that if God had really meant for us to see the sunrise, He'd have scheduled it later in the day.

This is not to say that I haven't ever seen a sunrise or that I've never experienced the other 5:30. I have. It's just that I tend to arrive at dawn by staying up rather than getting up. That's why it was so strange the Sunday morning I woke up at 5:00 A.M. and couldn't go back to sleep. I stumbled into my writing room and picked up a copy of what Mark Twain labeled "chloroform in print" and started to read.

Why is it, I wondered, that the lost souls get so much attention in the scriptures? If you're a prodigal son who comes home, your dad throws a party. If you're a world-class persecutor on the road to Damascus, you get a light and a voice. Even if you're a sheep that strays from the fold, the good shepherd leaves the ninety and nine good-guy sheep in search of the lost one.

The argument can be made that all of us are lost, and these stories remind us that no matter how far we've strayed or how far we've fallen, there's hope and a way back. These stories are *exactly* what we need to hear when we're feeling lost and alone.

But what about the people who aren't particularly lost but may feel unnoticed? What about the ones who are carpooling Cub Scouts, serving in the soup kitchens, taking clothing to Goodwill, donating blood, singing in the choir, volunteering at the hospital, visiting the nursing home, tutoring students, teaching Sunday School, coaching Little League, and doing the thousands of other activities the regular good guys do . . . without any spotlights or fanfare, without seeking any credit, without building themselves up? What about the ones who are wearing out their lives more or less being the kind of people the good shepherd doesn't have to worry about? What about them?

I was rather surprised at how intensely I asked this question and how quickly I got a musical answer.

I am one of the ninety and nine.
I'm not perfect, but basically I'm doing fine.
I have not lost my way, I have not gone astray.
I'm just one of the ninety and nine.
And I'm here in the heart of the fold.
I'm not mindless, but I try to do as I'm told.

I'm not tempted to run and become a lost one.
I'm just here in the heart of the fold.

So why is my shepherd coming this way toward me?
He's holding His arms out and calling my name.
He's calling my name, but how can this be?
I'm just one of the ninety and nine.
I have stumbled and fallen, but I've kept in line.
I'm not one He must seek; I'm not all that unique.
I'm just one of the ninety and nine.

So why is my shepherd treating me like His lost lamb?
He's searching to find . . . me . . . and He's holding me now,
He's holding me now, and teaching me who I am.
And why am I feeling like I'm the only one here?
It's like . . . it's like I'm His favorite . . .
And He takes me aside and He sweetly confides
These remarkable words in my ear. He says:

"You're one of the ninety and nine.
Have you any idea how brightly you shine?
You are safe in this fold
And it's time you were told that I know where you've been,
So I know where you'll be,
Because all of your life you've been following me.
You are more than just one of the sands of the sea
Or just one of the ninety and nine:
You are mine . . . you are mine . . . you are mine . . . you are mine."
Guess I'm one of the ninety and nine.

120

After I wrote this song, a new paradigm started settling in for me. I started seeing certain stories in the Bible revealing Jesus as being less critical than I used to imagine. For example, for years I thought that "Doubting Thomas" was a bit of a disappointment to Jesus because he was a fellow who couldn't just take somebody else's word for it. But now, I imagine the exchange between the skeptical apostle and the resurrected Master as being far more understanding and less critical of the personality that needed to see to believe. Remember, Thomas wasn't abandoning ship after Jesus died. He was just having a hard time putting all the pieces together. My new, post-Ninety-and-Nine feeling is that if we're doing the best we can and we need to see to believe, then surely we will see, if that's what helps us on our journey to follow Him. And if seeing is not that important to us because we have believing blood, other blessings will be available, as needed. Whatever blessings we need, we'll receive.

I'm feeling that wherever we are on the path, that's exactly where God will meet us and walk with us and teach us and encourage us and love us, if we'll let Him. If His burden is easy and His yoke is light, that's how He makes it so: He meets us where we are. In the fold or out, He lets us feel what perfect love feels like. Life is hard enough without our distancing ourselves from the One who has been willing to do whatever it takes to help us become all we have the potential to become.

I'm not sure how long it will be before I read these scriptural stories and see yet another way of thinking about things that I missed earlier. But I'm open and waiting. My promise to myself to follow those promptings and never pretend that I can do it all on my own is captured in a song called "Take My Life":

I took a snapshot of my life,
But the exposure was all wrong;
I couldn't see a thing developing.
It's been that way too long.
So I've come with a request,
Though part of me thinks I'm insane,
But I'm determined to see this thing through
And I will not complain.
Please take my life and turn it into something better . . .
Choose any way you will.
Take this shack, break down the walls and build a palace
Up on a higher hill.

I thought I knew where I should go;
I tried to get there on my own.
I took the easy roads, but now I know
That I'm lost and all alone.
So take my life and turn it into something useful.
Don't stop until you're done.
Take these eyes and make them see a clearer vision
Of what I can become.

And on those days when I feel like I'm dying
I'll trust in you and I'll keep on trying.
If you have picked this road, I'll take it,

And with you as my guide, I know I can make it.
Just take my life and make it one that is worth living.
Don't stop until you're through.
Take this life, the one that I am freely giving.
I give it all . . . to you.

CHAPTER 20

STAY WITH ME

It was my first trip to Nashville, and I had appointments with record industry people, genuine big shots. I was carrying a demo tape with my best songs.

This could be it: the big break. I bought boots.

The most important meeting was with a gifted and hugely successful producer named Jim Ed Norman. He'd produced all the big hits for Anne Murray, not to mention other legendary stars. A dear friend of mine had stuck his neck out for me and arranged for me to get to meet this man.

I knew Mr. Norman was extremely busy, so I decided to play only one song for him—a song I hoped Anne Murray, who was at the peak of her popularity, would consider singing. I was so excited for this opportunity, I didn't really notice that the new boots were so tight I'd lost all feeling in my toes.

There weren't many what you'd call "pleasantries" exchanged

with Jim Ed before he put the tape into his machine. He was busy. But I was pleased that the song sounded particularly good coming out of his sound system—even better than in the studio where we had recorded the demo. I was proud of the work but tried to act humble as the tune played on. It wasn't easy.

I tried to watch the producer's face, without it looking like I was watching his face, in search of clues: hoping to see if he was particularly moved by a lyric in the verse or delighted by the chord changes in the chorus. He didn't reveal much. Must be from years of experience playing poker.

When the song was over, he rewound the tape and handed it to me.

"No," was all he said.

What did that mean? No. I needed to know what he meant, so I asked him. "No, like the verse is too long, or no because the chorus isn't memorable, or no because the lyric isn't specific enough? What?"

"Just *no*."

He wasn't trying to be mean, I don't think. He was busy and not interested and anxious for me to leave.

"Look, Mr. Norman, it's such an honor to meet you and to have you take time to listen to my song. Is there anything you can tell me that would help me make it better? Any suggestions on what I should work on?"

"If I had the time to rewrite your song, I'd be better off writing one of my own. I don't know what else to say, but . . . no."

As Mr. Norman was handing me my demo tape, my friend

entered the office. Peter was always positive and extremely encouraging. "Hey, Jim Ed, the kid's got potential, don't you think?"

"I guess you could say everyone on earth has . . . potential."

I left the office devastated. I'd had a shot at presenting a song to a major player in the industry I wanted so much to be a part of, and he had hated it. How could he have hated it? Was it really that bad? And the hardest part was, I didn't have a clue how to begin to make it better. Maybe I was just one more of the pathetic dweebs who come to Nashville with unrealistic dreams, mediocre songs, and tight boots.

The flight home was eternal. I listened to the song over and over again, trying to imagine how I could have made it better. I couldn't. It was the best I could do, and that obviously wasn't good enough.

Not quite a year later, I was sitting in my office at a production company and the receptionist told me that a Glenn Yarbrough had come to see me. I wondered if this could be the same Glenn Yarbrough who had been a very successful folksinger with a group called the Limelighters, and then on his own as a solo artist. I hadn't heard anything about him for years. I'd thought he was dead.

Turns out he wasn't, and he had come to visit me because he'd heard I was a pretty good songwriter.

"Really?" I said a bit suspiciously.

"I was in town doing some concerts and thought I'd look you up and see if what I'd heard was true."

I took out a copy of the tape I had taken to Nashville and

threaded it into the machine. "Would you like to see a lyric sheet?" I asked.

"That's okay, I'll just listen." He closed his eyes when I hit the play button and didn't open them again until the song was over. He was in tears.

"That's incredible," he said. "What a gift you have. What else can you play for me? I've been on a sailboat for ten years and I've decided to come out of retirement and want you to write an album for me."

"Yeah . . . sure . . . whatever." I probably could have disguised my jadedness better, but I wasn't up to it. What did this guy want from me? He couldn't have been serious about the song. Something must happen to a person who drops out of sight for ten years and sails around the world on a handmade boat.

"I'll be in Reno at Harrah's with my band. I'll call you and have you come and see the show. Might give you some ideas for songs."

"That sounds just great. I'll wait for your call." This was not my most genuine moment. In my heart I knew something was wrong with this picture.

A few weeks later he called and invited Lynne and me to come to Reno to see his act. I never thought of myself as the kind of a songwriter who would flourish in casinos, but it was fun walking into the showroom as an invited guest of the headliner.

Midway through the show, Glenn said to the audience, "I'd like to introduce you to a great young songwriter who's with us tonight. If things work out, we'll be doing an album together soon. Please welcome Michael McLean."

It was like something out of an old black-and-white film on AMC. Unknown songwriter humbly stands in nightclub at the beginning of his rise to stardom.

Well, the stardom part never happened, and I'm not sure how humble the songwriter was, but Glenn was as good as his word, and I spent my thirtieth birthday in the studio with Glenn Yarbrough producing an album titled *Stay with Me*.

Shortly after the album was produced, I was watching a music awards show and saw that Anne Murray was nominated in one of the categories. Her record had been produced by Jim Ed Norman. I snarled at the television and hoped they would lose.

And then it hit me. Something was terribly wrong—with me and with the business I was in. Whom did I trust to tell me the truth? Whoever told me what I wanted to hear. Glenn was a great guy because he loved my songs; Jim Ed was Satan because he didn't. And yet the truth about the work, and about me, didn't change, regardless of whose opinion was being shared at a particular moment. The truth was something I knew, and I had to learn to trust it and to be willing to follow it, absolutely, or I would be lost.

I made myself a promise that night that I've been trying to keep, though sometimes I stumble and fall. The promise was that I would trust completely in the inner voice that always tells the truth. I would be grateful if someone were ever touched by something I had written, and humble enough to learn from those who weren't . . . but the final judgment about what I was working on would come from an incorruptible truth detector within.

"Stay with Me" was originally written as a love song, the pinings

128

of someone whose heart has been broken, yearning for a new love to stay with them just until their heart recovers.

Every story has an ending
Even when it can't be told,
And every broken heart starts mending
When it finds shelter from the cold.
I've heard a window always opens
When the doors have all been closed.
And though I know it's true,
Right now I need more light to see me through . . .
And oh, I need you
To stay with me
Just until my heart recovers.
Stay with me,
It's a lonely thing to suffer.
Tell me how the heartache I feel now will go away someday.
Maybe we just might find the answers that will carry me
Like an awkward dancer on a crowded floor,
I'll learn to dance once more someday . . .
If you'll just stay.

Life takes many sudden twists and turns that none of us can predict.

When I first started writing this song with my friend Chris Harding, I had no idea how it would be rejected in Nashville or later embraced by Glenn Yarbrough. I also didn't see that a rewrite of the song would be necessary to help some friends cope with the loss of their child.

Lynne received a call for us to meet our friends at the hospital. Their two young sons had been riding in the back of their car with the window rolled down to let in some fresh air. I don't know the exact details of how it happened, but apparently carbon monoxide was sucked into the backseat and both the boys passed out. The older child survived; the two-year-old didn't.

When our friends came out of the hospital to give us the news, it was devastating. Our children were the same ages as those boys. It could have been us. The grief was palpable in that parking lot. I tried to say something comforting, but it came out wrong. In moments of such sadness, I'm not sure if words are ever as needed as the silent, unspoken embrace.

Our friends did not have a lot of family nearby, and I was asked to prepare something for the funeral of their son. I didn't have to preach a sermon about forever, they told me, just help them get through *now*.

A few sleepless nights later I rewrote "Stay with Me" and sang it at the funeral.

I did not know that I would sing the same song the day my grandmother buried her son and grandson who died in an automobile accident.

It's interesting how my perspective about this song changed after those events took place. The question was no longer about how well the music was crafted, but rather how tenderly it might comfort those who needed someone to stay, just until their hearts recovered.

> *No one ever can be certain what another day will bring,*
> *So dim the lights and raise the curtain,*
> *The cast is waiting in the wings.*
> *Life goes on and on forever.*
> *And though deep down inside I know*
> *I'll have him back again,*
> *I'll still be lonely until then.*
> *And Lord, I need you*
> *To stay with me just until my heart recovers.*
> *Stay with me, it's a lonely thing to suffer.*
> *Tell me how the heartache I feel now*
> *Will go away someday.*
> *Maybe we just might find the answers that will carry me*
> *Like an awkward dancer on a crowded floor.*
> *I'll learn to dance once more someday*
> *If you'll just stay . . .*
> *And Lord, I know that you will stay.*

CHAPTER 21

BRIDGE OVER TROUBLED WATERS

In my dreams.

SHARE THE JOY

I'm worried.

I'm worried because there's a story I want to tell, but in the telling I might hurt some people. So I'm weighing whether the end of this story justifies the means of telling it.

Okay. I think there's a way of telling this so it won't hurt anyone. I'll lie. My justification for this lie is that I'm protecting the innocent, but we both know that isn't true. In one way or another, most lies are really about protecting ourselves. Besides that, the problem with starting a story with a lie is that it might infect the part of the story that's true.

I know what I'll do. I won't lie. I'll just tell the truth very carefully.

One of the not-so-neat things about being a songwriter is that being judgmental is an occupational hazard. It's the only way to make your songs better. You have to be willing to find the flaws in your own work and rework it a thousand times if necessary. However, sometimes this criticalness goes beyond your own work and eavesdrops on others. It's not a wonderful thing, but it happens. Upon seeing or hearing work that seems disappointing, a writer's trained instincts take over, and an internal editing process begins.

There's an old joke about a study that was done at Columbia University to determine the three greatest needs of mankind. The first (no surprise here) is the need to sustain life, to eat. The second is the continuation of the species—you know, sex. Those aren't really that earth-shattering, I know, but the folks at Columbia found that the third force that drives all mankind is the need to rewrite someone else's musical. I don't think they got that wrong. I say this as one who's been working on one musical for seventeen years . . . but I digress.

My true story is about a musical presentation that I was invited to see. It was the talk of the town, a daunting endeavor, to say the least, and it had been in development for years. I knew people in the cast, crew, and creative team that had put it all together. Friends of mine had worked very, very hard for a long time. I went to the production praying that it would be a huge success.

They didn't need my prayers. It was a big hit—sold out every night, held over by popular demand. Standing ovations, people in tears of gratitude for the experience of either being in or seeing this show. It was a triumph.

I didn't like it.

At first I thought the reason I didn't like it was because nobody had asked me to help write it. I think all creative people want to be asked to do everything, even though they know they don't have time and may not be the right person for the job. But that wasn't it. I just didn't like it, and as I looked at others during the show and spoke to many afterward, I realized that this program was connecting deeply with lots of people, just not me.

I started wondering what to think. What was wrong with me? Had I become so critical and weird that it had robbed me of the joy these other people were feeling? I started to question whether it was a good idea for me to continue in the field I was in if I couldn't even understand why people were so moved by something that left me so cold.

This affected me so deeply that I said a little prayer in my heart on the way home from the theater. The prayer went something like this: "Dear Heavenly Father, do you love this? Is this your kind of show? Am I completely out to lunch? Have you been trying to get me to appreciate this kind of work for years and I've been too stubborn or too proud to get it? If I have been wrong, let me know, and I'll change, but I've *got* to know: *Do you love this?*"

There was a real urgency to my prayer. Maybe that's why I got an answer so soon.

"I love them."

I was confused. This wasn't an answer to the question I had asked, so I asked again. The answer was the same: "I love them."

Why wasn't I getting the answer I wanted to hear: that the Creator of heaven and earth sees things the way I do; feels about things the way I feel; likes the same things I like. But He didn't go there. The answer was simply: "I love them."

Unable to get the Lord to critique and compare His children's creative efforts, I was forced to think about my question. Maybe I was asking the wrong one.

I know this may be a shocking revelation to those of us who have spent a bit too much of our lives in pursuit of validation through art, but the final judgment day will probably not be spent reading aloud to one another God's reviews of our artistic works. Maybe His perspective on artistic endeavors is, like most things at this stage of my life, beyond my current comprehension. And maybe His answer was simply trying to get me to ask the better question. I don't think I would have ever been able to articulate that better question had I not been told about a book by C. S. Lewis called *The Great Divorce*.

The book is about a fantastic bus ride from hell to heaven. In one of the chapters we get to see what happens to a man—a famous artist when he lived on earth—when he tries to stop the bus so he can paint a landscape in heaven. The Spirit who guides the bus tour tells the once-famous artist there's no need to stop and paint:

> "When you painted on earth—at least in your earlier days—it was because you caught glimpses of Heaven in the earthly landscape. The success of your painting was that it enabled others to see the glimpses too. But here you are having the thing itself. It is from here that the messages came. There is no good *telling* us about this country, for we see it already. . . . If you are interested in

136

the country only for the sake of painting it, you'll never learn to see the country."

[The artist protested,] "But that's just how a real artist is interested in the country."

"No. You're forgetting," said the Spirit. "That was not how you began. Light itself was your first love. You loved paint only as a means of telling about light."

"Oh, that's ages ago," said the [artist.] "One grows out of that. Of course, you haven't seen my later works. One becomes more and more interested in paint for its own sake."

"One does, indeed. I also have had to recover from that. It was all a snare. Ink and catgut and paint were necessary down there, but they are also dangerous stimulants. *Every poet and musician and artist, but for Grace, is drawn away from love of the thing he tells, to love of the telling till, down in Deep Hell, they cannot be interested in God at all but only in what they say about Him. For it doesn't stop at being interested in paint, you know. They sink lower— become interested in their own personalities and then in nothing but their own reputations.*"

As this is all sinking in, the once-famous earthly artist asks about meeting other artists on the journey, the really distinguished people. The Spirit's response jumped off the page and grabbed my full attention.

"But they aren't distinguished—no more than anyone else. Don't you understand? The Glory flows into everyone, and back from everyone: like light and mirrors. But the light's the thing."

"Do you mean there are no famous men?"

"They are all famous. They are all known, remembered, recognized by the only Mind that can give perfect judgment." (C. S. Lewis, *The Great Divorce* [Harper Collins, 2001], 83–86; emphasis added)

I can still remember how powerfully this passage impressed me, and upon rereading it, just now, I can't help but wonder where on earth I found the ego to even *think* I could write something on this subject when writers like C. S. Lewis have already said it so superbly.

In fact, if you're a writer who is wondering why this book got published and your manuscript is sitting in the drawer, you might be tempted to ask the heavens, "Do you love this?"

I suspect the answer will be, "I love him."

We all share the same sun
And we share the same moon
And we share the air that we breathe.
But we all share much more—
Every soul at its core
Knows what every other person hopes and needs.
Every heart wants to grow,

Every mind needs to know,
Every voice wants the chance to be heard.
Every person who lives—
Shares the hope they can give.
Let us all share the joy . . .
Share the joy.

CHAPTER 23

SOMETHING'S BROKEN IN MY BRAIN

P eople familiar with my songs are scratching their heads and wondering why they've never heard of this one. Answer's simple: As of this writing, I haven't recorded it anywhere but in my own head. There's been something about the process of reviewing the lessons my songs have taught me that has given me the courage to share this one.

I started taking medication for my depression after being unable to deal with it any other way. Diet, exercise, prayer, service to others, reading the scriptures, therapy, getting enough rest—all these good things were blessings in my life but not cures for my condition. I can't count the times I was overwhelmed with guilt for being depressed when I had been given so many wonderful gifts: a remarkable woman who loved me, great kids, a supportive extended family, an interesting career, and enough money to pay the light bill. What kind of creep gets everything on the Christmas list and then pouts in his room? An ungrateful little snit. (That's an *n*, by the way, and if you can't find the word in a regular dictionary, call my relatives, who have been identifying snits for generations.)

Somewhere in my messed-up brain I knew I didn't deserve all the gifts I'd been given, but to make matters worse, I was unable to find joy in the blessings.

It all came to a head when I was in New York City at a festival for new musicals. *The Ark* had been selected as one of ten musicals to be showcased in two off-Broadway theaters for producers and theater owners from all over the country. It was a truly thrilling opportunity, but I felt no enthusiasm for it. Only fear.

Fear because I couldn't remember things. Chords to songs I'd been playing for years escaped me. People I've known and loved, worked with and admired for as long as I can remember—I couldn't remember them when I saw them. Fear that the fraud police had finally received the warrant for my arrest as an impostor. Fear that I'd done nothing in my life, with my family or my career or my community or my church, that had made any difference at all. All those wonderful things people had been telling me for years were lies. Those folks were just being nice, but I knew what they *really* thought, and it wasn't good. All passion had faded; all self-confidence, fleeting as it had always been, was completely gone, and I was exhausted. A journal entry from September 29, 2000, gives a pretty accurate description of how I was feeling. The sad thing is, this was written on a "good day" when I had enough energy to actually write something down:

"I'm tired. Really tired. Don't think a power nap is going to cure this weariness I feel. It's a bone-deep kind of tired, and it's a melancholy kind of tired. I'm tired of being me. Tired of fighting the same battles with myself day after day after day . . . tired of carrying the same old burdens, same old struggles, same old hang-ups that have been plaguing me most of my life. There's something not right about the way I feel and I'm not sure what it is. Perhaps it's a chemical. Maybe I'm just lacking the serotonin (or whatever it's called) levels in my brain that would enable me to feel joyful, hopeful ABOUT ANYTHING, and not so tired. On the other hand, it might be behavioral. My actions, my lifestyle, my work, my schedule . . . all of this may be the cause of these feelings.

"I wonder if the chemical rush of my creative work and artistic lifestyle has given me a false sense of balance in the past. Maybe my overactive involvement in music, performance, writing, speaking, teaching, producing, selling has been my way to counter the feelings of weariness—emptiness that often overwhelms me—OR—the way I live my life is what has actually created the state I'm in. I don't know.

"In my heart and mind I know that my Savior and Redeemer is the One whose 'burden is easy' and whose 'yoke is light' . . . But learning how to transfer my burdens over to Him has been a bit of a challenge, to say the least. Truth is, I don't think I know how to do it. I HAVE experienced His loving comfort, and the easing of the pain, but I don't know what it was I did that helped that happen.

"If I say, in my prayers, 'I'm tired—tired of carrying all this baggage, could you carry it for a while?' I'm stuck by the feeling that after 'a while' I'm going to have to deal with some of those issues that I'm temporarily avoiding. That's part of why I came—to learn how to overcome these things—so I want help. I need help. But I also want not just to have my burdens carried by Jesus, I want Him to teach me, if it's possible, what He'd like me to do to reduce the burdens I may be creating in my life.

"It's good to know that I'm not carrying the burdens of grievous sins or unresolved wickedness from my past. I love my wife and children. I do pray, I walk the walk, keep the commandments, pay my tithes and offerings and try to do what's right—but perhaps there's something I'm missing. Sins of 'omission' unrecognized.

"I'm on a plane to Knoxville, Tennessee, where I'm scheduled to speak to a group of single adults. This event has been planned for months and months. I'm afraid these folks are about to hear from someone with virtually every blessing they've ever prayed for and yet I feel as depressed as many of them AND I HAVE NO EXCUSE. What's up with that?

"I'm tired of whining about all of this, even if the whining is only to myself. I'm sure that if I suck it up and focus on the task at hand and the service of others that much of this will ease up somehow. But my problem is that all this service and trying to give and share and lift up others seems, at times, like a foolish attempt to postpone facing that which is truly weighing me down.

"This weekend, the words spoken and the songs sung will be for me. Those songs have always been messages for my own heart—perhaps I should listen."

A week or two after I returned from that conference, the feelings of hopelessness and despair got darker and darker. My memory got so bad that I thought I might have Alzheimer's. I went to see my therapist and my doctor, skilled and capable people who cared about me and who suggested I try taking a pill. An unimpressive, tiny, pink pill. I didn't want to take a pill. What if I became hooked on some happy little drug and avoided facing the real issues of my life? What if it robbed me of my ability to think, and feel, and write? What if the price I had to pay for my art was this suffering? Would I lose whatever gifts I'd been given if I was medicated? What if "better living through chemistry" proved my greatest fear: that I was an emotional cripple who couldn't get through life without a crutch? The whole pill business scared me, but not quite as much as the thoughts I was thinking during my worst bouts of depression. So I took the advice of my doctor and my therapist and took the medicine they prescribed for me daily for four weeks.

Nothing changed.

This didn't surprise me, really. It was all too simple. Take the pill, the cloud will lift. Right. Surely there was more I needed to do. What kind of victory over this demon could I claim if all I did was take the pill?

And then, one morning, I woke up and something was different. It wasn't euphoria. It wasn't a rush. It wasn't like the end of a happily-ever-after movie. It was just . . . normal. It took a while to realize that this feeling, this normal thing, was real and could be sustained beyond a few fleeting moments.

I don't quite know how to describe what it was like to feel normal, or at least what I thought normal must feel like. I'm not sure anyone feels "normal," but for me it was sort of like this: level.

Everything wasn't always uphill or down. That pushing down, pressing, claustrophobic darkness was gone. I felt good when the sun was shining and sad when my friends were blue. I celebrated weddings and cried at funerals. I felt naturally excited about things that were worth being excited about, and not like the end of the world when I made a mistake. I could remember things, like the names of people I cared for and the chords to the songs I loved. The regularness of it all was and is simply wonderful. I'm amazed that somebody figured out how to do this for me and others like me, and believe me, I'm grateful.

But the lesson of all of this didn't begin to really sink in until I found myself scratching out some lyrics alone in my truck after a five-hour drive to a concert. The entire drive I marveled at the way I felt and had been feeling since the medication kicked in. The resulting song is a creation called: "Something's Broken in My Brain and Only Pills Can Fix It."

> Something's broken in my brain
> And only pills can fix it.
> I fought this thing for years in vain,
> Believing I could lick it.
> I tried and failed and felt so weak;
> It made me quite the cynic.
> And then I heard the heavens speak:
> "Mike, get thee to a clinic."
> I thought that meant the clinic
> For my own immortal soul,

145

So I trudged down to a church to wait
For God to make me whole.
Then something happened then and there
That came as quite a shocker:
I heard the voice of God say, "Mike,
I meant get thee to a doctor."
"But you're the God of heaven and earth,
My King, my Lord, my Master.
Why not just heal me here and now?
It's cheaper and it's faster."
He paused so long I thought He'd gone,
And then, in all His glory,
He shared an insight that will be
The moral of my story.
He said, "I whispered to some scientists who couldn't see
The one who guided their research was none other than me.
You see, I know you wonder
If I hear prayers when you say them.
Well, I've heard all your cries for help
Long before you pray them."

My gratitude for my pill has led me to believe, as the song suggests, that there's somebody in heaven who hears and answers many of our prayers long before we pray them. I also think that everything any of us has been given is meant either to help us personally or to be a means of helping someone else. Is it possible that many gifts are given to one person on a seemingly insignificant day that are really meant to be opened and used by someone else at some distant, giftless tomorrow? Perhaps the songs I write are my way of making deposits into some melodic bank account, all waiting for some future withdrawal. Hard as it is to imagine sometimes, I believe all of us can be the tools in heaven's hands to answer someone else's prayers. If you sense my optimism you have probably guessed that, yes, I took my pill this morning.

CHAPTER 24

THE MAN WITH MANY NAMES

I t was a tourist boat, made to look like a replica of the old fishing boats that once worked on the Sea of Galilee. I'm not sure how much it actually resembled the real boats, but having seen *The Robe*, *Ben Hur*, and *Demitrius and the Gladiators*, I was satisfied. It was good enough for me.

The weather was calm the day we were there. I tried to imagine the kind of storm that would have brought deep distress into the hearts of those disciples who followed the carpenter's son from Nazareth. I couldn't. But there's something that happens to you when you're in that place, that holy land, that changes the way you envision everything biblical. Being there causes you not only to see things differently but to hear things differently as well. In whatever tone I had heard the voice of the Good Shepherd before, I heard it differently in my heart and in my mind after walking where He walked and, on this particular day, sailing where He sailed.

The tour guide invited us to join him as he read from the New Testament the story of Jesus calming the stormy sea and walking on the water. I almost didn't open my Bible because I had already read that story dozens of times. I thought I knew it, and its meaning, by heart. A passionate disciple, Peter, sees his friend walking on the water, jumps out of the boat to greet Him, takes a few steps, and then panics and sinks. What I had always liked about the story was that Peter, a cherished friend of the Man from Galilee, could falter and receive a reprimand from the Master for losing faith. If Peter could blow it, I didn't feel so bad about myself and the times I had questioned and lost faith.

Moments before the tour guide began to read the account, something inside told me to listen up. My immediate response was, "Why? I know this story."

The inner feelings returned, whispering, "Listen up, Michael, you might learn something." That got my attention. I opened to the book of Matthew, chapter 14, and followed along.

"But the ship was now in the midst of the sea, tossed with waves: for the wind was contrary. And in the fourth watch of the night Jesus went unto them, walking on the sea. And when the disciples saw him walking on the sea, they were troubled, saying, It is a spirit; and they cried out for fear. But straightway Jesus spake unto them, saying, Be of good cheer; it is I; be not afraid.

"And Peter answered him and said, Lord, if it be thou, bid me come unto thee on the water. And he said, Come. And when Peter was come down out of the ship, he walked on the water, to go to Jesus . . ."

Reading along, I wasn't seeing anything new or profound. The story hadn't changed much since the last time I had read it. But just as we were about to read the part where Peter tries and fails to reach Jesus by walking on the water, the whispering voice inside penetrated even deeper into my own soul, with a real sense of urgency, and said again, "Michael, listen more closely. You might learn something."

At this point, the tour guide reminded us of the fact that the Peter we were reading about was actually named Simon, and that his friend Jesus had given him a nickname: *Petrus*, which means *rock*. For some reason, I imagined Peter looking like a Jewish Rocky: strong, intense, loving, and loyal, not a character from a fairy tale but a living, breathing human being. I looked out at the sea and imagined that person leaving us in the ship to be with his dearest friend.

"But when he saw the wind boisterous, he was afraid; and beginning to sink, he cried, saying, Lord, save me."

And then something changed me forever. I saw that "rock" sink, and I heard him cry out to his friend, and I felt the fear, and I didn't want to hear him criticized. I wanted to explain that Peter was just trying to do his best, that he was the only one passionate enough and willing to dare to reach out for his Lord. It was as if in my heart I was crying out to Jesus, "Go easy on him. He's just a guy who loves you so much. Don't tell him he's failed."

When the tour guide read the following words I braced myself, because I wanted the story to be different than I had remembered it. And the miracle is, it was.

"And immediately Jesus stretched forth his hand, and caught him . . ."

I saw it in my mind's eye and I started to cry. I wasn't sure why I was crying, except that I felt like I was there and I was seeing it happen in front of me. Then, as the words of the scriptures were read aloud, I heard a different voice from the one reading: "O thou of little faith, wherefore didst thou doubt . . . [that I would save you?"]

And then I heard a conversation that wasn't written in the book of Matthew, but it felt like scripture to me at that time. I heard Jesus explain to Peter that He wasn't disappointed in him for sinking in the water—that's what rocks do. He wanted Peter to know that no matter what the circumstances, no matter what the fear, no matter what the opposition, at the moment Peter reached out and cried, "Lord, save me," he would *always* be heard and rescued.

I then saw, in my mind's eye, Jesus holding Peter close, and they had words together that I couldn't hear. What impressed me was how close those two men were, embracing on the waters of the Sea of Galilee and talking as Jesus helped Peter back to the boat. I sensed a kind of love I had never before imagined between them. And I wanted it for myself, but I couldn't imagine ever being that close to the King of kings.

And then the voice inside said gently, "Wherefore didst thou doubt?"

At that moment, Jesus wasn't "out there" somewhere in the heavens, looking down on me, wondering when I was going to take a false step and blow it. He was next to me, holding me up, whispering in my ear, being the best friend I would ever have and making me feel as if He felt grateful to be loved by me, and not just the other way around. How could He be so wonderful? How could He be so real? How could He be so close?

Before my trip I had wondered why Jesus had so many other names:

Emmanuel, Wonderful, Counsellor, Mighty God, Everlasting Father, Prince of Peace, Stem of Jesse, Mighty One of Jacob, Servant of the Lord, the Messiah, the Messenger of the Covenant, Redeemer, Holy One of Israel, Blessed of God, Son of David, Son of Abraham, Son of Man, Jesus of Galilee, Jesus of Nazareth, Son of God, Nazarene, Only Begotten of the Father, Lamb of God, Meek and Lowly, Prophet of Nazareth, King of the Jews, Savior, Mediator, Light of the World, Bread of Life, Good Shepherd, the Way, the Truth, the Life, the True Vine, Rock of Our Salvation, First Fruits of Them That Slept, Forerunner, Advocate with the Father, King of Kings, Lord of Lords, Living Stone, Deliverer, Alpha and Omega, the Beginning and the End, the Word, the Almighty, Lion of the Tribe of Judah, Root of David, the Bright and Morning Star.

And then it dawned on me. He wants to be close to us. He wants nothing to cause us to think He can't relate to us, to our needs, to our challenges, to our experiences. And He wants us to know that He can be *everything* we need.

> *There is One who to this garden comes*
> *Like a most unusual rain.*

Drink it in and never thirst again:
Living Water is His name.
There is One who comes to find each one
Who has lost their way again.
He will lead the way back to the fold:
The Good Shepherd is His name.

There is One who, when your crying's done,
Gives the gifts you've never known.
He'll give fruit because He is the Vine,
And Life, for He's the Living Stone.
He is known by oh so many names,
And will be forevermore.
Hope comes from the One with many names,
And He's not forgotten yours.
No, He's not forgotten yours.

CHAPTER 25

WHO WILL BE THE REAL HERO?

𝄞

We got on the bus together and took the fifteen-minute ride downtown to see *Old Yeller*. To our way of thinking, it was the greatest movie about a dog ever made. *Lassie* had its moments, and *Rin Tin Tin* was a staple of Saturday morning television, but nothing was as good as *Old Yeller*. And no one was as much fun to see it with as my cousin Mark.

Mark was older than me by a couple of years, and when you're a kid you tend to look up to those who are a little bit older as if they were a lot older and smarter than you. That can make them kind of intimidating. But when the older cousin treats you like an equal, invites you to go to the movies on the bus with him, without grown-ups, you're bonded forever.

There was something pure about my cousin—not stuffy or self-righteous or weird, just pure. He wasn't natural to this earth. I always felt like he was a friendly alien, on loan from another planet populated by gentle souls with strong spirits and deep faith. He made this place his home for awhile, but this wasn't where he belonged. He probably stayed as long as he did for the rest of us.

No one thought he'd live that long. Born with diabetes, he wasn't projected to even see grade school. In grade school they doubted he'd make it through his teens. After he'd become an Eagle Scout, no one was predicting that he would serve a two-year mission for his church or learn to be a skilled surveyor and a craftsman who built his own furniture.

He was my favorite cousin to ride bikes with as a kid. He wore a look of perfect joy when he was soaring on his Schwinn on a summer day, shaded by the leaves at Liberty Park. He saw things around him that I think I missed, and he stayed a bit longer at every place we stopped along the way, as if he wanted to drink in just a little more. It was as if his whole soul were downloading crystal-clear images into a memory bank he would need to make withdrawals from in the future. Maybe that happened because he knew somehow that his lifelong illness would take his sight.

I never heard him complain about his blindness. I tried to get him to, just so I could feel better about my own outbursts of frustration for life's injustices. But he wouldn't go there.

"Of course I miss seeing, Mike. I was a surveyor by trade. I loved working with my hands. But now I see other things."

"Like what?"

"Like goodness. Like when I'm waiting for the bus and people ask if I need a lift. They want to help. And I don't have to see things that kill the spirit anymore. Violence on TV. Degrading, awful pictures. Not a part of my life."

"But still . . ."

Mark finished unscrewing the bolts of the front wheel of a ten-speed bike and placed them in a special place near his workbench.

"It's teaching me patience, that's for sure. Learning Braille, finding a new career, figuring out how to keep track of things you can't see, like these wheel bolts. All courses in the school of life."

"I don't think the line for those courses is very long, Mark."

I found myself pacing around. Rocking back and forth. Checking my pocket for my keys. Looking at my watch. If he could have seen me, it would have been clear to him that I was getting increasingly uncomfortable. Even though he couldn't see, he could tell.

I said, "I couldn't do it. It'd kill me."

"No. You'd adjust. Who knows, you might even write better songs . . . look at Stevie Wonder."

A gentle soul with gentle humor, but not a weak one. Not by a long shot. This guy was tough, mentally and physically. He had disciplined himself to keep track of things, and he also worked on keeping himself in shape. Hugging Mark was like wrapping your arms around a rock that hugged back. Even when they started amputating his toes, and then chunks of his foot, he stayed strong in spirit and body.

He never complained, right up to the end. Of his three beautiful children, he saw only one. The other two, including a daughter who looks just like him, he would have to imagine.

156

He never complained. He kept trying to be all he could be, and never whined and moaned when his personal dreams were altered. He wasn't perfect; it just seemed that way to me because he mastered long ago so many qualities I'm still struggling to develop.

When we let him go, I had the great honor of singing at his funeral. As I sang, I saw him riding his bike with that sweet smile on his face. His eyes were open wide and he was drinking it all in again. He was going so fast that the wind was blowing his hair back and billowing his jacket. He was going downhill. After a lifetime of climbing to the top of the mountain, it seemed only fair.

Who will be the real hero when the race has been run?
Who will be the real hero when it's all been said and done?
Will it be the one who gave us everything he had to give?
Those who would be real heroes know how real heroes live.
There's a part of them that's knowing
There's a price that must be paid,
And they know that when the going gets rough,
A hero's made.
Heroes know it's not the cheering of the crowds that gets it done.
Heroes know the real victories in life are one-on-one.
There's so many souls in need—
Who will have the strength to lead and
Be our real hero when the race has been run?
Who will be our real hero when it's all been said and done?
It will be the one who gave us everything he had to give.

157

And in our hearts, somewhere, forever,
All the real heroes live.
And in my heart, somewhere, forever,
Our sweet Mark will always live.

CHAPTER 26

HOLD ON, THE LIGHT WILL COME

I've done a lot of talking in this book about letting go, but I'd like to end it by talking about holding on. I'm not sure which is harder. I suppose it depends on what you're needing to hold on to or let go of. I wish we were chatting about this, one-on-one, instead of me doing all the talking. All these personal stories to the contrary, the truth is that I'm much more interested in what you think and have to say than in my own musings about the eternal verities. Let's think of this as my part of show-and-tell, and because of the wonders of technology you can take your turn next. It's easy to get to me. My website is MICHAELMCLEANMUSIC.com. If you write, I'll respond.

I wrote the song "Hold On, the Light Will Come" in a dark hour. That may be why it means so very much to me. I had been working on a musical about Noah's Ark and was trying to come up with the perfect song for Noah to sing to his family after it stopped

159

raining. In my own life, it had been raining so hard for so long that I didn't know what to do. I tried to ignore it, hoping it would just go away, but it wouldn't.

Someone told me once that heaven answers our prayers when the last amen is uttered. I felt like I was at a point where praying about a particular problem I was having was just plain stupid. I'd prayed it all a thousand times. If He wanted to answer me, He could. What was the point of making the same petition over and over and over again? Not knowing what else to do, however, I kept praying.

I looked for evidence that my requests were being heard. I looked everywhere and I looked long and hard. Nothing. I tried different approaches to my problems—read the books, talked to the people, listened for wisdom, and prayed at different times, in different places, and in different ways, hoping that heaven would open up and hear me. At last it came to a point where I just couldn't do it anymore. I gave up. I made my giving up a formal thing. I announced, prayerfully, that I was no longer going to pray about this specific challenge *that was killing me,* in case He hadn't noticed, and that I wasn't mad about the lack of response, though I had been before. I was just exhausted.

I didn't feel any particular peace when my last amen was spoken, nor did I feel flooded with hope and reassurance. I was just done.

There's a problem with "being done" with God, however, and that's that He's never done with you. While you're busying your life with activity to fill the void, He's busy preparing you for the perfect moment in which He can manifest the very love you are denying by "being done."

For me, it was a drive down the canyon. The sky was overcast, like my life, and an unusual melody started to fill my mind. At first, I could hear it but couldn't sing it back to myself. It was in a musical language that I didn't understand but that was more moving than anything I'd ever heard with my ears alone. I wished I could translate it into a tune I could understand, but I didn't have the skills.

"What is this? I love this. Why can't I sing it?"

I felt a peaceful invitation to simply listen for a while. I didn't need to think about how I could translate this into a song. I just let it speak to my soul.

So I listened. The tune was accompanied by lyrics in yet another language I didn't fully comprehend. It was a language of the heart and it pierced me to the very center. Whatever it was saying to me was beautiful, but I couldn't share it with anyone, and I suppose I wasn't supposed to.

I just listened.

I remember thinking how much I didn't want to forget what I was experiencing, but I had no tools to remember this song, so I just tried to hold on to it . . . appreciate it . . . hear it . . . feel it . . . receive as much of it as I could, and trust that that was enough.

What I was desperately trying to hold on to was the hope that whatever this was I was feeling, it was part of my answer. I remember saying "thank you" over and over again, in a whisper, as the song without comprehensible words or melody just filled me to overflowing.

When I got to my office, I sat at my piano and played the opening notes of a new song. It wasn't the song I'd heard in my head. I couldn't re-create that one if I tried. That one was way beyond my abilities. But what flowed from me was my song of gratitude, my humble effort to put into my own musical and lyrical language the smallest part of what I'd been given.

> *The message of this moment is so clear,*
> *And as certain as the rising of the sun:*
> *When your world is filled with darkness, doubt, or fear,*
> *Just hold on, hold on,*
> *The light will come.*
>
> *Everyone who's ever tried and failed*
> *Stands much taller when the victory's won.*
> *And those who've been in darkness for a while*
> *Kneel much longer when the light has come.*
>
> *It's a message every one of us must learn,*
> *That the answers never come without a fight.*
> *And when it seems you've struggled far too long,*
> *Just hold on, hold on,*
> *There will be light.*
>
> *Hold on, hold on, the light will come.*
> *Hold on, hold on, the light will come.*
> *If you feel trapped inside a never-ending night,*

If you've forgotten how it feels to feel the light,
If you're half crazy thinking you're the only one
Who's afraid the light will never really come—
Just hold on, hold on, the light will come.

The message of this moment is so clear,
And as certain as the rising of the sun:
When your world is filled with darkness, doubt, or fear,
Just hold on, hold on . . .
The light will come.

A few years ago I had an opportunity to sing this song in New York City at a workshop for musicals I was invited to attend. Each night of the workshop, writers would present portions of their musicals and then have them critiqued by industry professionals. Another way of explaining it is that Broadway legends would listen to your songs and give feedback. Basically, you got beat up by really smart people.

On one of the evenings I had a chance to share some songs from the show we were working on about Noah's Ark. "Hold On, the Light Will Come" was the last one I sang. Afterward, everyone took a break before the second half of the workshop was to get under way. While I was milling around, trying to grab what looked like the most perfect oatmeal raisin cookie I had ever seen, someone approached me.

"You don't sing, do you?"

"No, not really. I guess tonight the idea was that the writers would just share their work themselves."

"Well, I've been to all the sessions of these workshops, and usually we hear Broadway stars singing all these songs, but tonight . . . well, tonight you . . . you . . . you know, you really can't sing."

"I really heard you the first time."

The awkwardness that I thought was the natural result of such New York bluntness ended up being about something else entirely. This guy pulled me aside from the rest of the group so he could say something he clearly didn't want anyone else to hear.

"Could you answer something for me?" he asked.

"I'll try."

"Tell me, what was it I was feeling when you were singing that I wasn't feeling when the real singers were singing?"

His question was direct and sincere and didn't seem to have any kind of hidden agenda. I wasn't really sure how much of an answer he wanted from me, and I didn't know how much I could share with him in that setting. The Mormon in me wanted to say, "Well, I've got a couple of friends who'd like to come over to your house and talk about that feeling," but I didn't. I just asked him what he thought it was, and he said he wasn't really sure, but it felt like something. Then the crowd dynamic moved him away, and we didn't continue our conversation.

I wish there had been time for me to tell him that I think what he might have been feeling was that same thing I was feeling driving down that canyon—and those feelings weren't from the song. They were from the Master Orchestrator of our lives, the Man with Many Names, the One who is the source of all light, all hope, and all truth. And when He sends us those feelings, often when we're listening to music, it's to remind us that the greatest songs have yet to be written and the greatest melodies have yet to be heard. They're out there waiting for us to listen closely enough to hear them. And once we've truly heard them, we can never be the same.

If you haven't heard yours yet, hold on, the light will come. I don't know where you'll be or how you'll hear it or when you'll feel it, but it will come. It has to come. In fact, it may already be there.

Just listen.

CODA

𝄋

If heaven will send coded musical messages of hope to help out a depressed, middle-aged father and balding songwriter on an alfalfa farm, then surely there's something uniquely on its way to you. And my guess is, it will be exactly what you need.

If any of these stories and their accompanying songs have found their way into your heart, I want you to know that I *know* where they came from. I don't say that pretentiously or because I think I'm some unique conduit for inspirational songs. But if you felt something in them that's different from a lot of the things you hear on the radio, I think we both know what's been going on.

One parting thought: You've got so much music inside you that is crying to get out. You have songs we need to hear and to join you in singing. You may not know a treble clef from a meat cleaver, but that music is in there. Your unique songs may not have conventional melodies or words, but when they come from that place that is authentically and completely you, there will be a new harmony that wasn't there before. Don't give up, don't give in, don't be afraid. Sing that song of life only you can sing.

Someone's listening.